At Whitt's End 2

A Continuation and Collection

of Narratives and Poetry,
Random Thoughts and Short Stories

Janean J. Phillips

Cover illustration by Craig V. Thomas

Printed in the United States of America

First Printing, 2017

ISBN 978-1-945091-25-4

Ordering Information: Special discounts are available on quantity purchases by bookstores, corporations, associations, and others. For details, contact the publisher at sales@braughlerbooks.com or at 937-58-BOOKS.

For questions or comments about this book, please write to info@braughlerbooks.com.

**Braughler
Books**
braughlerbooks.com

This book is dedicated to my children and children-in-laws, and granddaughters, to my friends, to my dad Charles, and my 8 brothers and sisters.

A special Thanks to my brother Brian, my brother John, my friends Christine, Robert, Mike, Viv, June, Lorraine, David, Kathy, Barb, William, and to all of you, who have supported me, encouraged me, and stood by me, along the way.

God bless you for letting me be a part of your lives.

This is Dedicated to Everyone, because
EVERY Body HAS A STORY:

These are Random thoughts and Random stories in no
particular order, from my youth, or from just the other day,
so to speak, because I have a lot to say...

Some are conversations with family and friends, regarding
physical and emotional obstacles...in Narratives, Poems,
Prose and Short Stories... Some are very adult, some are
juvenile, and some are very direct and blunt...

This book is dedicated to everyone with whom I spoke, and
with whom I did not get a chance to speak to in person,
who are fighting the truly awful battles of the physical and
mental, which in turn causes additional internal emotional
battles of faith, spirituality and hope.

Some of these stories are of fighting, of truth, of praying
and hoping. I have been open to the idea of praying and
receiving messages that will help me find my way as well.

Not all things turn out as one wants or hopes, however, in
my opinion, if you are willing to be open to alternative
thoughts, alternative physical methods, in addition to faith,
hope and prayer, one may at least live the rest of their days
in peace and contentment and in harmony with what has
been dealt.

Some of the things that I have learned in my life are: Do
not be afraid to ask for help. Do not be afraid to reach out
to others like yourself. Talk out your sadness, vent to
friends and family and counselors. Meet new people and
know that they, too, have some sort of battle.

Keep a journal. Jot down your dreams, despite how bizarre they might be...

Write often and always. Take a daily walk (if it's not a blizzard out there). Train, and run a marathon. Push your physical abilities to its limits. Absorb nature.
Volunteer. Pray.

Experience the little things and appreciate those little things that make life worth living. If possible, go on a cruise, travel, take a dedicated friend, or just hang out at the local tavern, with friends and family, laughing about childhood stories, share a joke, or laugh at what makes you sad.

Invite friends over, have a small party, watch a comedy, eat whatever you want.

Along with those things, take close-up pictures of yourself and others, take close-ups of dandelion seeds, an ant in the grass, a sunset, a spider web, a single grain of sand...
Pack a swim bag, put on your swimsuit, go swimming, even if only in your own bathtub.

Make a photo album or scrapbook.

Write your own eulogy.

Say what's on your mind and think about how you would like to be remembered.
Cry often.
Write...
This is your life. One life.
And...

Every BODY has a story...

MY BROTHER, BRIAN

Shhh. Don't tell anyone, but my brother Brian is my
favorite sibling, out of my eight brothers and sisters.

Since he is right above the first set of twins...and I am in
the middle of the two sets of twins, I think perhaps we have
felt like the odd men out. I can't speak for him, but I have
felt that way from time to time.

As we get older, life happens. We meet our future beaus
and girlfriends. We meet our future spouses, we get
married and extend our families. No different than the rest
of the people on the planet, one by one, each of us, all nine
kids to be exact, did just that...and moved out
and moved on.

Life happens. Gaps occur. Fights break out.
Misunderstandings rear their ugly heads.
Gatherings become more difficult as time passes.
Marriage. Children. Jobs. Loss of jobs. Loss of wages.
Friends. Enemies. Travel. Food.
New jobs, new friends, new locations, new homes, new
beaus, new girlfriends, new spouses, new children, school,
college...
Bills. Cars, car insurance, car repairs, duct tape, use of the
barter system to get repairs repaired. Car tags, car stickers.
Adult beverages. Health. Health insurance.
Trips to the doctor.
More trips to the doctors, the specialists and memorizing
the names of the nurses.
Disability. Privacy.

The desire to NOT be a burden to anyone.
Personal battles. Prayers. Faith. Renewed faith.
Hope. Love. Dedication. Cherishing your loved ones.

The realization that time is not on your side.
The realization that time is running out.
The realization that you are not going to live forever.

**I hadn't seen Brian for many months, say, for many
years, when our mother got sick, she was transported to the
hospital and eventually died that next day.
A dreary November day, indeed.
But running into Brian, was as if time had never passed.
We were in a hospital, specifically the hospital
Consultation room, which by the way, was too small to
house all nine of us, plus our spouses and children and plus
our dad.
Brian and I quietly joked about how hungry we were, when
friends of our family brought in bagels and cream cheese.
We were sitting side by side, on the dinky couch, our heads
almost touching, looking at each other slightly giggling.
One other sibling made a comment that our behavior was
"inappropriate." That made us giggle all the more.
Here we were, in a hospital, with our mother dying in the
next room so to speak, with other siblings and in-laws
crying, worrisome, nervous, "besides themselves," as my
mother would say...and we were deciding not to discount
our individual hunger.
So being me, unafraid to dive into free food, I challenged
him to which one of us would get up first. He chickened
out and I got up, but he followed suit...and so did everyone
else. I am a trend-setter. Plus I love bagels and cream
cheese.
As we ate, we did our best to get caught up with each other
and everyone, quietly of course. Obviously, I will never
forget that day, especially, seeing my children and my
brothers cry. I was the only one brave enough to be with
Mom in her room, as the nurses turned off the machinery.

Eventually, other things happened, and our mother passed away quietly, but that is another story.

I met with Brian on July 3rd, 2015. I drove from my home in Ohio, with my two granddaughters in tow, took them back to Tennessee to my daughter, visited for a bit, then made my way back up to Kentucky to interview my brother, a survivor of cancer.

He and his wife Beverly and teenage son Jared were there, adding to the details of when his illness began. I couldn't get out of the car fast enough, to hug them all. Birds were chirping in the trees. I heard the sound of the loose gravel under my car tires as I pulled into their driveway. The mid-day fog was still settling on the mountains and valleys surrounding their modest home.

It had been raining the entire trip to Tennessee and then to Kentucky, but for the brief moment of me exiting my car, and grabbing my brother, the rain had stopped and left a haze and a bit of humidity in the air.

He was still frail from the surgery of nearly four years earlier, that took half of his tongue and all of his teeth, but never took his will to live...and his determination to fight this somewhat hopeless battle.

Their dog jumped up on me, leaving a dirty paw print on my new jeans. None of this seemed to matter to me, whereas in the past, it would have.

I am not sure why, but I love the sound that my shoes make on a wooden porch, and their porch supplied that wonderful childhood memory, of my grandmother's home in West Virginia. An additionally welcoming sound echoed from my childhood, as their screen door made a clap sound against the door frame as we entered their living room. We sat in the living room and talked, then moved to the kitchen, and I became increasing aware that this day may be the last day that I might see him.

This is his story, in his truthful words:

It was the second week of April in 2011. I had pain on the right side of my mouth. Even after several days, it didn't get any better. The aggravation of it went on for days and days. I brushed my teeth a lot more and used more mouth wash, but the pain never went away.

Once I saw my family doctor, he touched my tongue and the pain was excruciating. He just came out and said, "I think you have cancer."

*Beverly commented, "After Brian found that out, he called me and told me that he had cancer. I asked where he was and was mad that he was on his way back to work."

I was sent to a specialist by the end of April, and he found a tumor that was far back into my tongue and jaw. Within two months, I had seen the specialist again, and it had advanced from Stage Two to Stage Three Neo-Plasma Malignant Tongue Cancer.

Since I had found out that I had cancer, I was more nervous, and I smoked a lot more. But on the day of the surgery, I wasn't too nervous. Dad was there, and he told me that I showed no fear. Dad asked me if I was afraid and I told him that I knew that I had to have it done. I had to trust in God and trust in the surgeons.

The surgery and plastic surgery took place on June 28th. I was put into a medically induced coma, eventually given a feeding tube the day before the surgery, and was not allowed to have a nicotine patch because nicotine restricts blood vessels. Ever since the surgery, I have lost a total of 40 pounds.

Back in April of 2006, my doctor found a spot on my back, the size of a fifty cent piece. He removed it, via an outpatient procedure. It, too, was cancer.

For my tongue surgery, they had to cut from my bottom lip down to my chin, crack my jaw open, cut most of the way to my ear along the jaw line and clip the bottom of my tongue for access. The doctor said it would be like carving a turkey, piece by piece, in order to remove the cancer. They removed 33 lymph nodes, leaving a big divot in my neck. They sent sections of my tongue and surrounding tissues and muscles to a lab. They had to remove more around the tumor to make sure they had it all.

I remembered waking up in my hospital room and seeing this one poster on the closet door. It said: "Know your rights as a patient." I couldn't talk, I would fade in and out of consciousness, and all I could see was that poster. Once I was able to fully wake up, I was trying to communicate, trying to write on a pad of paper. All I could write was "Ibu." Beverly knew that I wanted more pain killers, like Ibuprofen.

Two weeks to the day of surgery, I left the hospital with post-surgery instructions, to take care of the wound and take advantage of the in-home medical care. I had two-thirds of my tongue removed, they reshaped my tongue from a graft on my right wrist. This type of cancer has an 80% chance of reoccurring.

In four years, I've had 4 PET scans and so far, no more cancer. I also had several Radiation treatments since the surgery and 6 surgeries, and I have had speech therapy. My doctor said that my drinking and smoking is the cause of my cancer.

In the Spring of 2012, we went to our tax preparer, to do our taxes. When we told her about my cancer and surgery, she stated that I was lucky, so I asked her what she meant. She told us that her husband had had the same cancer and had died with only 2 years notice...that he never drank and never smoked... The fact that he died did not make me happy, but made me think that perhaps my doctor was not entirely correct.

That made me think about a previous job that I had had, as a spotter for a tanker truck company, where I would be inside the tanker, cleaning out tanker sludge, sometimes without a mask. I had had that job in the mid 1990s.

In December of 2011, I had to go back to work. I've been fighting Social Security for quite some time, because currently I am not in a position to work. I am taking 16 different prescriptions, I don't have any teeth, it's hard to understand my speech sometimes, I've lost a lot of weight. The plus side is that I am eating better and have gained 10 pounds in four years. In the winter of 2012, I contracted shingles, perhaps because my immune system has been damaged or at least affected. Even now, I am still fighting the SS Department because I cannot function, I am worn out daily and my eyes feel too heavy to stay awake.

Ever since the surgery, the skin around the metal plate behind my bottom lip would not heal properly. I was sent to Wright Patterson Air Force Base Hospital and was put in a barometric chamber to get the wound to heal from the inside. My jaw bone was exposed and would not heal. Ever since the surgery, I have nerve damage on my right side of my jaw, and despite the radiation treatments, I can grow hair on my chin.

In June 2014, the area around that plate formed some scar tissue, but still wouldn't heal. While at work, it busted open and I had to be rushed to the hospital for an arterial bleed surrounding that plate. The doctor said that it was a matter of time that the scar tissue would snap, that it was like "a baseball hitting a glass window." At the ER, the nurses were in a panic because they could not get my mouth to stop bleeding. I was practically bleeding to death for an hour.
The ER doctors were thinking of cauterizing it through my thigh. Eventually my plastic surgeon came in, said NO, and was able to stop the bleeding within 10 minutes. He

stitched it back up... Even during this life and death
moment, I lied to the doctor about smoking.

I must admit that even on the day that I left the hospital for
the first time...after my initial cancer-removing surgery and
tongue removing surgery, I wanted to smoke and I had tried
to smoke, even with a swollen face.

**That statement came as a surprise to me. I must admit
that I did not know that, and that I had a better
understanding of the hold that this horrible addiction had
on my brother.

In December of 2013, we moved to Kentucky. The tube in
my belly fell out on its own, whereas the opening healed
itself from the inside out. In June 2014, I had a colostomy
reversal. That doctor looked at my belly and said it was
fine and as long as I wasn't in pain. He didn't see a need to
cut me open again, to fix it from the inside. The area still
leaks occasionally.

**Once we were done talking about Brian's cancer and
surgery, we moved to the back porch where we took photos
together and chit-chatted about our brothers and sisters and
about Dad. We reminisced about some childhood stories,
talked about my children and plans for the next day's
holiday, July 4th. Brian told me that he appreciated the fact
that I was willing to drive them up to Ohio and that he truly
wanted to visit, but long drives hurt his back. He has
bulging discs and it hurts to sit for long periods of time.

I watched and listened and pondered why the two of them
still smoked.
I thought of the garden that I saw out front.

I thought about myself for a moment and some of the medical woes that I have encountered throughout my lifetime...
I watched as their dog was playing in the yard of their neighbors two houses over...and I became a bit overwhelmed, having a need to leave, so I could bawl in the car on the way home.

What is this devil called Cigarettes that has a clawed grip so strong on this man...whom is loved by his wife, loved by his son and loved by his family? What can be done to get rid of this vice, completely and for good, so as my brother can heal? Can he be stronger than this? What happened to this strong man, whose once stocky body has become frail? What other Godly truths can he believe in, have faith in, so he can find peace and contentment for the rest of his life?

Days after I had gotten home, I started writing this story, and it took me more times to get it started. I kept crying...and I am crying still.
The moment that I had gotten home from interviewing him, I made my required phone calls to my children and to dad, then one to Brian, to let them know that I made it home safely.
Brian had called me the next day, telling me that they had fallen asleep early and that he had heard my phone message that morning. Being me, I took this as an opportunity to further my interrogation...I mean, interview...
We talked about some steps that he could take to stop smoking. I mentioned about finding something to replace the urges, like taking a walk and meditation, as well as identifying the urges, writing in a journal, focusing on his garden, making money by "renting out" garden space to his neighbors, etc. I am sure that I was getting a little loud, but I held myself together, knowing that I was angry for no reason. He is quite aware that he is still smoking...

I told him not to be shocked when and if his son starts
smoking. I told him that he and his wife will continue to
fail at stopping, if they are not supportive of each other.
I asked him this one question: If there is one thing that you
could tell your younger self, what would it be?
His answer: Definitely to NOT start smoking.
I told him that I loved him, that I hoped to see him again
real soon. He told me that he loved me, too...and I knew
that to be the truth.

MENOPAUSE PAUSE

I can't believe that I have to pee again in the
middle of the night,
And I scared myself in the mirror,
for I looked such a fright.

I am gonna blame it all on this menopausal Bitch,
Which is also to blame, for another mysterious itch.

I think that it's got to be another yeast infection,
Whereas it makes me feel like I am less than perfection.

Over time, my hair has gotten so much grey in it,
I am coloring it red again, so as to look younger and fit.

But I am not fooling anyone, just myself and him,
I am running extra miles, but I am not feeling so slim.

My arms are saggy, so are my tiny boobs and my belly,
He doesn't seem to mind, because he likes peanut butter
and jelly.

I am a wreck dealing with aging spots and aching feet.
I am not happy with the hot flashes, nor all of their heat.

Just as much, I am turning up the radio,
because now I can't hear,
Just like my grandmother, I'm calling everyone
"Sweetie" and "Dear."

In daylight, I look into my mirror and see myself as a kid,
I see myself capable of doing everything that I once did.

But, the sounds that my body makes is quite realistic,
and funny.
Even he can't remember my name, because
he keeps calling me "Honey."

I will feel more content, whence this menopause will cease,
He and I will rock on the porch, and we will finally have
some peace.

RANDOM THOUGHTS, at this ridiculously late hour:

*I haven't been up this late in eons because I'm feeling
old most days, this includes on
New Year's Eve, Saturday Night Live, the Super Bowl,
the local news, etc...
*I had a latte at 9am, which is probaly why
I'm still awake...
*I still hate the snow...
*I'll take 60 degrees in February...
*Anyone wanna bet me a dollar that I'll still wake up
around 6am, because heaven forbid that I'd sleep in?...
*Completed online courses for work for the past 5

and a half hours, earned 2 free items...
*I lost four lbs this week, ironically and obviously,
from eating more, and eating healthier foods...
*An apple a day probably does keep the doctor away...
*I need to remember to play the lottery...
*I need a vacation...

A PATHETIC ATTEMPT AT THIS HOLIDAY POEM

As I arise this morning, I can honestly say,
That I truly, 100%, dislike this day.
For many a-year,
Valentine's Day,
Has sucked anyway.
If I'm gonna get dinner, chocolates and flowers,
It'll be me doing the buying.
I'll just keep trying, to keep myself from crying,
With all of the sighing, and the past wishes of dying...
Red might be the color for This day,
With cardboard boxes, roses and ware.
I scream silently that it's just not fair,
And I tell myself that I really don't care,
So I continue through life with the red dye in my hair.

PAIGE
(Here is a long, short story that I started, just after my
divorce)

The front door lock was frozen. "Damn." She tried the key
in the lock several times, with no luck of getting inside.
The night air was cold on her face and she dreaded the
thought of being outside any longer. She set down her bags
on the porch and went to her car to find the safety kit.
"There it is. Right in the back where I left it." She
slammed the back hatch door and headed back toward the
cabin. An uneven walkway stone caught her foot and she
tumbled forward. "Damn it. This is what I get for coming
here." She got up, took a deep breath, and walked gingerly
to the front door.

That deep breath brought a memory instantly to her mind.
It was the night that she and Jordan had made love in their
back yard, under the winter sky. The children were asleep,
it was almost midnight, and the moon was almost full.
Jordan told her that it was the perfect night for "doing it."
He had teased her, in his pretend Renaissance voice, that
they must shed their clothing first and go to a forest with a
blanket." "We don't have a forest, dear," she sarcastically
had told him. He told her to just play along... "Okay," she
said. He continued, "We must walk side by side to the lake
and lay our blanket gently on the Earth. This is where we
must make love. We will be one with the Earth and sky."
Paige had played along and responded with a playful
accent, "Yes, we shall be in harmony with the stars and the
Earth." They stripped and ran as fast as they could, naked
in the moonlight, threw down their blanket on the hard
ground and made love. Jordan was very thorough that
night, along with most nights. He was not selfish by any
means and he was the most wonderful kisser. The night
was cold, but they didn't notice for long.

When she realized that she had been daydreaming, Paige
looked up to the stars and smiled. A shudder went down
her back from that memory.

Paige sprayed the lock with the deicer that she had found in
the car kit. That worked, so she turned the key and pushed
the door wide open. It was dark. She picked up the rest of
her bags and walked inside. Feeling the wall to her right,
she was able to locate the light switch and turned it on. The
light was overhead, attached to a ceiling fan. The globes
were dusty, one was not working, but the other three were
bright enough for her to see. The natural wood smell inside
the cabin made her nostrils flair. It was a wonderful smell.

She placed her bags down, turned to close the door and
gazed over the front porch. The moon was barely shining,
in the pitch black sky. Strips of clouds danced off the
horizon and floated away to nothingness. Several patches
of clouds remained in and around the moon, teasing the
onlooker by occasionally hiding it. It was serene and
almost completely quiet. The wind was blowing and the
trees gently swayed. The limbs cracked and rubbed against
each other, forcing tiny branches and twigs to fall to the
ground.
When the moon could be seen, its shine glistened on the
snow and on the lake. The snow began to fall and dropped
into the lake like shredded coconut. Paige walked to the
edge of the porch, looked up and caught a few flakes on her
tongue.

Retreating inside, she headed for the kitchen which was
directly across from the living room. She peered into the
fridge. "Good. At least the movers remembered my food."
She paused. "Am I really hungry? No. Just something to
do with my hands." She closed the refrigerator door. She
walked slowly around the entire cabin and walked toward

the potbellied stove in the center of the living room. She
gently caressed the flat top and lightly moved her fingertips
across, as if expecting it to be soft. That stove reminded
her of the one in her grandmother's home in West Virginia.

Her grandmother would tell her, "The stove will remain hot
for a long time after the fire is out. This stove has been an
important part of our family. We have always gathered
around it in cold weather. We eat by it, we dry our cold,
wet feet by it...and your grandfather and I, God rest his
soul, even made love by it." "Grandma!" Paige had
exclaimed. "Don't tell your Ma that I said that." "I won't
Grandma."
"Let's hold our hands as close to it as possible," her
grandmother would say, "Don't get burned. This stove is
like love, staying warm forever."

"I will remember you, Grandma, with this stove here."
Paige walked toward the bathroom at the back of the house.
The door was partially open. She reached in, turned on the
light and immediately noticed the vanity was slightly dirty.
"Movers." She opened a small storage door, got out a
towel and began to clean the surface. When she was done,
she looked up and stared at herself in the mirror. "Paige,"
she asked, "What are you doing here? Don't you know that
it is not safe for you to be by yourself? You might actually
get lonely, ya know." She stared a bit longer. "What have
I done? What was I thinking? A beautiful home, beautiful
landscape and no one to share it with..." She stuck her
tongue out at herself, pulled her short curly, red hair away
from her face and turned away.

She opened the corner shower door, looked inside, then
shut it. She walked a bit further into the bathroom.
Toward the left and behind the shower wall was the toilet,
and the washer and dryer beyond that. Against the right

side wall was the deep whirlpool bathtub, in the almond color that she had ordered from the dealer. It was the right size that she needed and the one that she had always wanted. There, would be where she would spend most of her days, getting away from it all. At her first home, with what seemed like light years ago, was where she had spent most nights in the tub with Jordan, after his long days at work.

That could be as relaxing as ever. Jordan's strong body was very comforting and felt good against her small frame. She remembered those moments with such deep appreciation. Any memories of Jordan, recently, would make her happy for at least a little while.

She made her way back through the living room and almost tripped when she came to the step leading down into the small, sunken second living room, at the west end of the cabin. She approached the fireplace and glanced over the pictures of her family. There was Jordan and Paige, in one frame, at their home in the backyard by the lake. The next picture was of Dean and Sarah, her two small children, nagging each other, in their original family room. And then the last frame was only of Paige, brightly smiling but looking a bit old and worn out from raising two over-active kids. Oh, how she missed her beautiful children.

Her lip began to quiver over the thought of never seeing her kids again. She closed her eyes to gain her composure. Paige continued her search throughout her new home, as if she was looking for something specific. "Something is missing," she thought. She almost became dizzy as she frantically looked for it. She hurried to her bedroom, threw open the door and sitting on top of the bed was the plaster hand-prints of Dean and Sarah.

"Why did the movers put them here?" she wondered. She gently picked them up, went back to the mantel and put them in their proper place, right next to the framed picture of her kids. "This is where you belong," she said aloud. "They belong here, next to their creators. This is exactly where they were, placed on the mantel at home." She put a kiss on one of her fingers, and placed that kiss on each of the hand-prints.

Paige decided to retreat to her bedroom. She was exhausted from the long drive from Ohio. It had taken a longer time to reach her cabin than she had previously remembered. The road seemed to be endless. She realized that getting in her car and leaving her home was now permanent. She had a hard time letting go of the place that she and Jordan came to fall deeply in love with each other, where they had raised their kids, had wonderful, caring neighbors and most of all, leaving her family. That was difficult for her, for they were very close. She felt as if she was always going to have those fond, childhood memories to get her through anything.

Paige knew that she was going to miss her most favorite of holidays, Thanksgiving. That was the best time ever, with her family. Everyone would gather at her parent's home, help prepare the entire meal together and also bring some kind of covered dish. Each of them would tease the other of which one was the best. It was a crazy and fun time, with different conversations going in different directions. Only those in-laws, who came from large families as well, would fit right into the chaos. If a new beau or girlfriend, who may have been shy, would come to visit, they would have possibly gotten lost in the shuffle. However, the best memories for Paige were meeting new people and making sure that everyone felt welcomed.

She came to this cabin to get away from the pain. Away
from the pain, sorrow and shattered friendships...the ones in
which she had counted on the most. This move was a
milestone for her, an itch that would not go away. She had
to do this. She would not be able to look at anyone again,
because of her guilt and shame. She blamed herself for
everything that went wrong in her life. Even when she was
little, if she had stubbed her toe, it was her fault. If the
flowers died in the garden, it was her fault. Since her
beloved family had died, she continued to wonder why she
was spared. "Why was I spared?"

Her undying guilt was what drove her these days. She
knew that she must be in control now. She needed to be in
control of everything. By being in solitude, she believed
that she was in control of her own destiny. Living alone,
she thought, was the only way to not be hurt, not hurt
anyone, and the only way to regain her sanity.

She looked at the clock and it was 11:30 P.M. She laid
down on the bed, with her shoes still on, her glasses still
on, and as she fell asleep, she pulled a fluffy blanket around
her shoulders. Her body and mind were exhausted. Now
she could possibly sleep, uninterrupted...

The sun shone brightly through the bay window in her
bedroom. Paige rolled over onto her back, realizing that
some time in her slumber, she had curled up into a little
ball. She was in a bit of pain. Her back was tight from the
uncomfortable position that she had allowed herself to lay
in overnight. She sat up in bed, stretched her back out
slightly by slowly leaning forward, then stretched her hands
to the ceiling. Moaning loudly from the stretch, she
scooted toward the edge and slowly stood up. She stood
for a minute and glanced at the clock on the hutch across
the room. She turned around and found her glasses on the

bed, which had come off during her sleep. She stared at the clock again, saying aloud, "Six twenty seven A.M. I cant believe it."

"What shall I do today?" Paige went to the bathroom, peeled off her clothes, only to her bra and panties. She started the shower, and let it come to her desired temperature. She looked into the mirror, brushed her teeth and smiled at herself. She pulled out a towel, from the shelf that was over top the washer and dryer. She felt a small twinge in her back and rubbed it. She said aloud, "I must have this looked at... But I don't know anyone in town." Paige didn't want to go to town. She wanted to remain in her cabin, away from civilization, forever. That was almost impossible and she knew it. She would have to find food, she would have to buy more wood for the fireplace and so on. She knew that that was the reality, but she just didn't want to face anyone.

She undressed completely, and stood in the shower, allowing the hot water to soothe her body. She stood motionless for quite some time. Realizing that she was getting light-headed, she quickly cleaned up and got out. She dried herself off, wrapped the towel around her body and went to the bedroom. Having a little trouble deciding what to wear, she finally settled on jeans and a simple long-sleeved pink cotton top. This little ensemble was her most favorite, for it was the most comfortable. She felt no reason to get too dressed up for anything.

She went back to the bathroom, hung up her towel, sat on the edge of the toilet and put on her shoes. She headed for the kitchen, because she knew that breakfast was what she needed to get her day started. She made scrambled eggs, toast and juice, and sat down at the dining room table, adjacent to the kitchen. That small, confined area was one of the attractions of the cabin that got her attention, when she was shopping around. She never really liked the large dining room at her other house. It felt too much like a royal palace dining room, that took one forever to reach the other side. She always loved petite rooms, where she felt close to the person sitting across from her.

Paige finished her meal, put the dishes in the sink and retreated to the small sunken living room. She approached the bookcase, selected The Great Gatsby, plopped down on the sofa and began to read. A bit later, she looked up from her book and realized that she was cold. She went to the front window and saw that it was fiercely snowing. She rushed to the fireplace and frantically started a fire. She felt a bit stupid, for not thinking of doing that first thing, when she got up. Lately, she was not doing a lot of smart and obvious thinking. She was in survival mode, which made her feel out of control. That was a feeling that she never liked.

As the fire finally started to grow, she sighed, "Ah..." The flames grew higher, then she replaced the screen back to its proper place. She started a second fire in the potbelly stove. She knew that those two fires should be enough to keep her warm for quite some time. She went back to the front bay window and sat on the sill to watch the world. A deer dashed in the distance. She watched it, as it disappeared from her sight. She had been holding her breath and finally let out a sigh. She continued to watch, as a small group of geese flew overhead. Paige became warm, from the fire and from the thought of the approaching season. Winter was never her favorite, but the thought of just staying put and just being an observer, from the inside, was quite fine with her.

Paige shuddered at the thought of possibly freezing to death. She hated that idea, for herself and everyone. She hated that thoughts like that just seemed to pop into her head, out of nowhere. She worried about people that she didn't even know, who didn't have a place to live, who were possibly homeless and may be out in this dreadful storm. She would even sometimes get sick to her stomach, from watching the news about crashes and the like, especially in bad weather. She believed that this over-empathic part of her was quite the curse. She even got sad about people that she would never meet.

As she sat on the sill, her mind continued to become jumbled. She thought of how, on some days, she would feel lucky than most...then on other days, how much she hated herself because of all the horrible crap that had happened to her. She had recently thought of committing suicide. Only just a thought, she thought. She reasoned with herself, that everyone thinks of doing that, from time to time, especially in distress. She wondered, "How can I think that I have it all that bad? I had a wonderful husband, I had two wonderful children, and I had a job. A job I hated, but a job, indeed. And here I am, sitting here, feeling sorry for myself." She said aloud, "I cannot afford to feel this way. I will die and no one would care. No one."

Paige slid off the sill, sat back down on the couch and returned to her reading. She snuggled into the corner of the couch, wrapped an afghan around her feet and savored the words that were in front of her. A few hours went by, then she finally put the book down. She went to the kitchen. She said aloud, as she placed her hands on her belly, "If I don't watch it, I will easily overeat and put on too many pounds. But why should I care?" She popped popcorn in the microwave, put it in a bowl, got a pop from the fridge, grabbed a napkin and went to the main living room and turned on the TV. She looked at the clock and it was now 4:00 P. M. She could not believe how fast the time had gone. She thought that she could not last too long staying indoors, that she would easily lose her sanity, if she didn't come into contact with others. She wondered what she could do to keep her mind off of her family. "What can I do to occupy my time out here?" she asked aloud.

All that Paige could find of decent interest on TV were Westerns galore. "There's always a Western on TV," she thought. She settled on one, curled up again, with her popcorn, and the afghan that she had knitted with her own hands. Soon her eyes became tired and she fell asleep. As she drifted off, she said a small prayer, to please allow her not to think of Jordan and the kids. She was so tired of waking with tears in her eyes, after seeing her kids dancing in her dreams, after spending time with the love of her life, making love at home and after seeing their twisted bodies in her mind... She wanted to erase those horrible images, but she didn't know how.

As Paige began to wake from her slumber, she realized that she was slightly shivering. Her cover was on the floor, the popcorn bowl was empty, but she didn't remember eating all of it. She sat up and saw that the fire in the stove was out. She rushed over to it and added more wood. She thought, "How in the world am I supposed to maintain a fire, let alone two of them? This is harder than it looks. I'm just gonna have to keep an eye on both of them, adding wood by the hour."

It was only 10:30 P. M., she observed, so she went to the kitchen, with the afghan wrapped around her shoulders. She found a piece of paper and a pen and jotted down her thoughts. "Let me make an agenda for myself."

She wrote: Get up. Do stretches and yoga. Bathe. Eat.
"What next?" she asked. She continued to write: Read a
book.
"Oh, Jordan would be so proud of me. I never had time to
do that. I'll read a book every day." Then she wrote: Go to
town. "Should I?" she asked aloud. "Maybe they won't
like me. Why should I care? I've never cared before.
You're just paranoid. I will pick up a few things at the
market, pick up a few newspapers to see what's going on in
the world, inquire about a local doctor for my back, then go
see him or just come back home. All of that should be just
so simple. It should be. This is what I will do tomorrow, if
I feel up to it." "We'll see," she thought, "We'll see."

Paige went to her bedroom, undressed from her simple
clothes, put on comfy pants, thick socks and an Ohio State
University sweatshirt, then quickly brushed her teeth. She
went back to check on both fires, checked all of the
windows and doors, turned off all of the lights, then
plopped down into her bed. "I will get a good night's sleep
and start the day anew. I've got to keep busy." While
laying on her back, she placed her hands together in front
of her heart and mumbled a simple little prayer, "Please let
me think of something pleasant tonight. Please no
nightmares, no guilt..."
She rolled over onto her side, placed a fat pillow behind her
back, curled the comforters and blankets up around her
chin, and fell asleep. After Jordan's passing, she had put a
pillow behind her, to trick her mind into thinking that he
was pressed up against her, so she could try to sleep better.
Some nights it worked, and some it did not.

Paige's nightmares began soon after the death of her family.
As she had gotten older, she knew that death was
inevitable, but she always hoped that she would have had
more time. She knew that everyone felt the same, thinking

that they had more time to live and travel and do things
with their families. In her mind for days on end, that day
played out, over and over again. She constantly questioned
herself, if she had told them that she loved them on that
day. Her mind was never settled from that question. She
knew that death was inevitable...but she never dreamed in
her worst nightmares, that death would find all of her loved
ones at the same time.

Her earliest reality of death showed up when her
grandmother had died, and even then, she was too young to
remember and too young to understand. Once she came to
understand the concept of death, she made peace with it,
continued to pray on it and she attended church regularly,
with the plan of seeing God, when death found her.

Why did it have to happen with her entire family? "Why,"
she murmured, as she drifted off to sleep...

As Paige was in between awake and asleep, she thought she
had heard something, or someone, come into her bedroom.
"Paige, wake up." It was Jordan. Paige glanced up,
"Jordan, what are you doing here?" she asked.
"I am here with you now," he said.
"How?" she asked...
"Paige, why didn't you come along?"
She heard the echoes of her children's disembodied voices
repeat, "Why didn't you come along, mommy?"
"I had things on my mind. I didn't want to go to the
movies."
"I know, but you should have come with us," Jordan said.
"You should have died with us."

Paige sat up. She had sweat and tears dripping down her
face. "Damn it!" She wiped the tears away from her face,
got out of bed, grabbed the comforter and went to the bay
window in her bedroom. She curled up on the sill, sat there

for the rest of the night with her face pressed against the cold glass, and fell asleep.

When Paige awoke, she was still curled up the same position, but with her face practically glued to the window. She somehow knew that most of her nights would be like that one, sleeping in the window, on the couch, or even in the bathtub. She never seemed to have the bad dreams until she was cozy in her bed. She decided that that was what she would have to do until she got comfortable with her new surroundings.

She forewent the idea of maintaining the fires...she took a shower, got dressed, ate a breakfast bar and had some juice. She sat down on the hard bench by the front door and put on her coat, boots, hat and gloves and grabbed her car keys from the nail on the wall by the front door. She opened the door, took a deep breath and ran out to her car. She was shivering, but happy that it was not snowing. She started the car and ran back inside the cabin. For a moment or two, she lightly bounced up and down to keep warm. She looked out the front window, found the thermostat and saw that it read 11 degrees. "Yuk," she said aloud.

After a little bit of time, she grabbed her purse, went out the front door, locked it, then darted to her car. Once inside, she turned on the defrost, looked around and finally found the car scraper and brush. She got out, dusted off the car, sat for another moment inside the car and finally put the car in Drive. According to her realtor, the road from her cabin lead right into town. She had told Paige that the little town wouldn't be hard to find. So, Paige took her realtor's word for it and headed in the right direction, hoping that the previous night's snowfall would not have covered up too much of the road.

The drive took about an hour, as the roads were not cleared. On the drive, she saw no one. She assumed that it would

have taken less time in better conditions. She saw tiny
houses, far apart, on lots of tiny hills. She saw a couple of
deer in the distance, but couldn't tell if they were real or
statues. The sky was heavily overcast, grey and dim. It was
a dismall day. She hoped for a better outcome, of running
into a few people, if possible. Paige wanted to play it safe,
but didn't know if she could contain herself, by not telling
too much about herself and where she lived. She knew
better than to let others know, strangers know, that she was
alone in a cabin, miles from anywhere.

As she ventured slowly into the small town, she saw a
courthouse, a post office, a police station, a vet's office, a
bakery and a flower shop, a tavern, then finally the market.
"BrownStone Market," she said out loud. She thought that
she may need to check out the police station, to introduce
herself, before she headed home. "Where in the world
would a doctor's office be?" she wondered.
The road was snowy and muddy. She parked in the lot next
to the market. She immediately noticed that there weren't a
lot of cars, but the majority of vehicles in the lot weren't
cars at all. They were all trucks or vehicles with 4-wheel
drive. "I need to get me one of those," she said aloud,
seeing a shiny black Hummer, as she exited her car. She
was glad that the lot was not full. When she went inside,
the first thing she heard on the PA system was "I Love a
Rainy Night." She began to hum along, as she got a cart
and began walking down one of the aisles. As she took her
time looking over some of the items, she looked back at the
cash registers and found it odd that no one was there.
There was no one in the customer counter booth either.
"Where is everybody?" she wondered.

She went up and down the aisles and found items to put in
her cart: multi-grain bread, eggs, crackers, a box of hot
chocolate, a block of cheese, peanut butter, almond milk,

soup... She stopped again, as she noticed that the song was over, but no other song began. She cocked her head sideways, in order to listen closely...to hear something, but there seemed to be no sound whatsoever. The hair on the back of her neck began to rise and she wasn't sure of what to do next. Was she asleep? Was she imagining things? What was going on in that store and why was it so quiet?

All of a sudden, the PA system screeched, then a loud metal-sounding bang. A man's voice came on the PA, "Sorry folks. We are having electrical problems. We will get the system back up and running soon." The male announcer did not realize that he was still on the air, as his next statement made Paige laugh out loud. "Wanda, I told you to stop drinking by the radio! You keep spilling things and I can't afford to have you do that again!" Next, Wanda commented, "Dennis, I told you that I needed to take a break and dammit, I am gonna take it here!...Oh my god, are we still on?" Then there was another loud bang and then the music came on. This time it was "Harper Valley, PTA." Paige almost doubled over in laughter. She heard other patrons in the other aisles laughing as well, making her realize that she was not alone after all.

As she rounded the corner of one of the aisles, her cart ran into another patron's cart. It's owner was standing in front of one of the frozen food doors, so Paige moved the cart a bit, in order to get by. She apologized out loud to the man, as he turned to see who had bumped into him. As she said, "I'm sorry," she looked up at him and he back at her, they got a puzzled look on each of their faces.
With a furrowed brow, he asked, "Where do I know you?"
"I'm not sure, but you probably really don't," she quickly and witily responded. They lightly laughed. He got a bit closer, but oddly, she didn't back up. Paige felt like she had recognized him as well. She realized that she had been

holding her breath, for he was quite the attractive male.
She had gotten a quick waft of his wonderful musky
cologne. He had brown hair, blue eyes, was just a bit over
six feet tall, she guessed...and man, oh man, he made
Paige's heart skip a beat, for a brief moment.

Paige was not prepared for that reaction. No one had made
her feel that way, except for Jordan. They began to get a
bit more close, taking guesses on where they knew each
other: Grade school? No. High school? No. Work...at
various jobs? No. College? No. In their childhood
neighborhoods? No. Paige told the handsome fellow that
she grew up in Ohio, and he stated that he grew up in the
New England area. They even took a moment to shake
hands, slowly, and introduce themselves.
"Hi. I'm Kurt."
"Hello, I'm Paige."

Hmmm... They were puzzled. Then suddenly, the answer
hit both of them at the same time. Simultaneously, their
eyes widened and they each took a step back. They had
realized where they had known each other before, their
faces lit up, then shock took over. "Time and pain can be a
heartless bitch," Paige thought.

Paige rushed past the man, pushing her cart with full force.
His reaction was lacking, for he turned in slow motion, to
watch her round a corner and disappear. Kurt was shocked
about running into Paige, and murmured, "Of all the damn
places in the world..." Paige took off for the checkout aisle.
She tossed her few items onto the belt and told the cashier
that she was in a hurry to get home before the pending
storm. "But the storm is already here," Paige thought. The
cashier looked at Paige funny, tried to make small talk, but
Paige ignored her. She had gotten her bank card out and
annoyingly tapped it quickly onto the small checkout

counter, looking over her shoulder and then back to the cashier.

It was evident to the cashier that Paige was nervous. "I hadn't heard that there was a storm coming. I thought we had gotten all of our snow last night, for the week." Paige had no reaction to her silly comment. Paige had gotten all the more agitated, as she felt that the cashier was taking her time, on purpose. Paige heard the clunk and clatter of the wheels of an approaching shopping cart. She was so nervous, that she decided to take off, "Oh, never mind." She clung onto her purse strap, ran out of the store, and ran as fast as she could toward her car. The cashier yelled out to her, "Ma'am? Where are you going?"

Throughout that passing moment, Kurt stayed put. He was still shocked from running into Paige. He placed his back against the cold door of the pizza selection fridge. He closed his eyes and let out a huge puff and sigh. He raised his chin, rolled his eyes to the heavens and asked, "What were you thinking? Why would you do this to me...and her?" He gathered his thoughts and his grocery cart, and headed for the checkout. Kurt was aware that he was on the verge of tears, but thought that a man should never cry. He gathered his composure before he approached the cashier.

The loud-mouthed, immature cashier was talking with her register neighbor. Kurt overheard that Paige had left in a hurry, as the cashier held no words back, describing her disdain over her leaving all of the groceries behind. Kurt offered to pay for Paige's groceries, as he paid for his own. He asked the cashier to bag all of it up, which she did. Her demeanor changed, as she smiled and flirted with Kurt. The other cashier came over and helped bag up all the groceries, and placed them in Kurt's cart. She, too, was

admiring Kurt's gifted looks. Her admiration was not
hidden at all. Once the transaction was over, the cashier
smirked at Kurt and said, "That's very nice of you, sir. At
least I don't have to put all of the stuff back." Kurt replied,
"No problem, but you should watch your mouth. I'm sure
your boss wouldn't mind to know what you just said about
one of your customers. Perhaps you should consider
another line of work. Say, like, fast-food, to go along with
your fast tongue."
He smirked as he left, feeling vindicated and harboring a
little bit of guilt. The two cashiers' jaws nearly hit the
floor, as Kurt turned on his heels and walked out. He could
feel their shock, even as he exited the front doors.

As Paige ran to her car, she had slipped on the snow and
slightly slid under the driver's side. She was so
embarrassed. Luckily, no one saw her, as she quickly got
up. She brushed off her butt and hips, adjusted her coat and
got into her car. As she was placing her key into the
ignition, she slumped over the steering wheel and started to
cry. She took a deep breath and quickly recovered, as she
sat straight up, placed her fists at her temples and yelled
out, "What were you thinking?" She started the car and
took off toward home.

Kurt took his time, as he put the groceries into the cab of
his truck. He was deep in thought. It started to snow. He
looked up and said, "Great." A sarcastic tone was present.
Just before he had gotten into his vehicle, he saw a purse on
the ground across the parking lot. He knew right away that
it belonged to Paige. He walked over, picked it up, and
brushed the snow off of it. He hesitated on what to do next.
He knew where she was staying, not because he was a
creep, but because everyone in that town knew everyone's
business. There was a-buzz about, earlier in the week, at
the grocery store, at the local diner, at the post office, etc.,

about the new owner of the cute, little, abandoned cabin in
the woods. "What am I supposed to do now?" he
wondered. "Why would fate bring us together...and why
now?"

Kurt sat in his truck, with the engine running. A few
minutes later, he made a phone call to the police
department. Clerk George answered the phone. Kurt could
hear him slurping on his coffee.
"Hey, George, it's Kurt. How's it going?"
"It's going okay. What about you?"
"I'm good. Hey, I found a purse in the grocery store lot. I
know who it belongs to, but I'm not sure if you'd rather that
you take it to her and not me."
"Who is it?"
"It's the new lady in town, who got the abandoned cabin.
Whatcha think?"
"Well, no one is here now to help. Ya know I gotta stay
here and answer the phones. A purse is not important. We
won't be able to take it until tomorrow, but I'm sure that she
is needing it. You know women and their purses." They
both laughed. "Are you okay to deliver to her now, if
you've got the time?" asked George.
"Sure, I guess." Kurt sighed. "I'll leave now. Just wanted
to let you know, in case she calls you and asks about it."
"Okay. I don't have her number, but just in case she calls,
I'll note the time. Thanks and be careful, Kurt. The snow
is picking up now."
Kurt replied, "Thanks, George. I will."

As Kurt hung up, he took a deep breath. He rolled his eyes
as he put his vehicle in Reverse, backed up and drove out
of the parking lot toward Paige's cabin. He dreaded seeing
Paige again. "I can just drop it off on her porch," he
convinced himself. "It's the right thing to do." He took his

time on the drive, knowing that the roads were slick, and
feeling that he was just not in such a rush.
His thoughts drifted as he drove. It seemed as if the snow
was putting him into a trance. His mind wandered to his
chance meeting of Paige, just moments earlier. His mind
concentrated on that brief moment of their carts crashing
into each other...her smile...her apology...and the sweet
smell of her flowery perfume. He had focused in on her
mouth, as they asked each other where they had met. In his
mind's eye, she was talking slowly, methodically...as they
giggled and guessed.
He quickly shook himself to reality, as he remembered her
face, at the moment that they had realized their identities.
He refocused on the snowy road. He restraightened his
truck, as it almost went off into a ditch.
Kurt's mind continued to drift...about the day that changed
his life forever. It was years earlier, he was tired from
work, and he had briefly fallen asleep at the wheel, when
he collided with another vehicle...

On the drive home, Paige was all a-fluster. She talked
aloud, repeating her disconnected thoughts, "What is going
on? Why here, why now? I just can't believe it. I don't get
what you want. I can't believe that I left my groceries. I'm
gonna starve to death. Damn, where is all this snow
coming from?"
None of what she was blurting out was making sense to
her. She was so upset, but knew that she needed to focus
while driving. She hoped that she was going in the right
direction, and hoped that she would not miss her own
driveway. She continued to drive slowly, then saw the
property's mailbox. Once Paige had gotten to her cabin, the
snow had been coming down full-force.
She parked the car as close to the cabin as possible. She
turned it off and quickly turned to grab her purse in the
passenger seat. She slammed her right hand down on the

seat. "Oh my god. Where is it?" She looked in the floor
boards, behind the seats and again in the floor boards. "Oh
my god. I must have forgotten it when I fell. Crap! What
do I do now?" She hesitated for a moment, then restarted
the car. She put the car in Reverse and high-tailed it out of
the driveway.

Kurt was just about to pull into her driveway, when he saw
Paige pulling out in a frenzy. Her car was about to hit him.
The road was slick as he swerved to miss her. She
slammed on her brakes, but not in time. Her car tapped his
truck and his truck flew uncontrollably across the road and
down an embankment. He could not control it.
Paige gasped as she witnessed what was unfolding before
her eyes. Her car came to a stop, she jumped out and ran
down the hill after the careenning car. She hesitated, to get
her footing, when she saw Kurt's truck head for a grove of
trees. She yelled, "Oh no," and continued to run down the
hill. The snow was slick, preventing her from running
faster. She watched as the truck veered to the left of the
grove and slid into a small pond at the base of the valley
below. "Oh my god!" She slipped and landed on her butt.
She slid down the hill and was able to slow herself as she
got closer to the pond.

Kurt swerved, but not fast enough to avoid Paige hitting his
truck. He felt the "thwack" of Paige's vehicle against his.
He chuckled as he thought, "So this is it." As he careened
down the hill, he thought it was comical that he continued
to hold onto the steering wheel. He was feeling that it was
a sense of security, although he knew he wasn't in control
of anything at that moment. Despite that, he couldn't let
go. There wasn't any time to do much of anything, but
watch what was happening.
He giggled uncontrollably, then got a feeling of
seriousness, as he felt that he was surely going to die. He

briefly worried about hitting his face into the wheel, hoping
not to break his nose, or knocking himself unconscious.
The scenery before him was breathtaking. Although it was
snowing and he was speeding downhill, it seemed as if the
sun was shining and that he was moving in slow motion.
He sat upright for a brief second, gripping the wheel even
harder, as he thought that he had heard a couple of voices
in unison. The voices were of children.
"Hold on, Kurt," the children whispered. "Mom is gonna
need you, too." Kurt shook his head, as he tried to dismiss
what he thought he had heard. He came back to reality, as
he heard Paige yell, and as he felt his car veer left and
plunge into the pond...

Paige caught up to the car a few moments later. Time
seemed to be frozen, just like the ground and the hazy air
that surrounded them. The front tires and a portion of the
front of the car rested at the bank of the pond, which
cracked through a thin layer of ice. Without hesitation,
Paige rushed into the water, pulled opened the driver's side
door and was happy to see Kurt uninjured. Kurt was a bit
shaken, but otherwise unharmed.

She breathed a sigh of relief. Kurt apologized to her, for he
felt as if the accident was his fault. "I'm so sorry," he
repeated. As she helped him out of the truck, she told him,
"It's okay. It's all okay." Both of them felt out of breath.
They helped each other, by getting a grip onto the frame of
the truck in order to pull him out. Paige reached around his
waist and grabbed onto the waistband of his jeans and
pulled with as much force as she could muster.
"Oh my god, the groceries," Kurt exclaimed. "The
groceries? Who cares about the damn groceries," Paige
responded. "I've got your purse in there." "My purse?"
Kurt reached back into the truck and grabbed her purse. He
handed it to Paige. She helped him out of the vehicle. Kurt

said, "Let me get the groceries. The truck isn't gonna move." "How do you know?" Paige asked. "I fish here a lot,"he said, "The bank flattens right here."

Kurt reached into the back of the bed of the truck and started pulling out the bags of groceries. He handed them, one by one, to Paige. Paige accepted them, placing them one at a time onto her left forearm. By then, the two of them were nearly knee-deep in the unforgiving cold water. They were freezing, their teeth were chattering and Paige was shaking uncontrollably. When they were done, they turned and headed back up the hill. Kurt stopped for a moment, looked into his truck, saw that there was water in the floor boards, and murmured, "Damn." They trudged up the hill, warming up a bit as they climbed. Periodically, Paige would look upwards toward the road. She thought that it was a miracle that he had survived, for the distance in which his car went out of control was quite significant. It took them several minutes to get to the top. Luckily, they were alright, she thought. It was still snowing relentlessly.

Once to the top, they got to her car, which was half-cocked in the middle of the road. They piled all of the groceries in the back seat. Paige turned on the car and blasted the heat. They sat inside the car for a moment and looked at each other. "Perhaps I should drive you to the hospital, to make sure that you are okay." "Not necessary. I am fine. A little shaken, but okay," Kurt said. He felt a sincere compassion from Paige. He could see in her eyes that she had genuine concern, as her brow was a bit furrowed. "Are you sure? Did you hit your head?" she asked in a shaky voice. Her teeth chattered as she spoke.
"Surprisingly, no," he responded. He was also a bit surprised that he hadn't really gotten hurt at all. She questioned him, by not saying a word, but by leaning her head to one side and giving him a stern look. Kurt smirked.

She sighed, "Okay," then drove the short distance to her cabin. The heater was warming them up a bit, but they were still quite uncomfortably cold.

With groceries in tow, they rushed inside the cabin. Paige asked Kurt to put them in the kitchen, as she ran to the fireplace, tossed in some wood and started a fire. She ran to the potbellied stove and started another fire there. All the while, Kurt was in the kitchen, putting away the perishable food. Each task took a few minutes, as neither of them questioned the other. It just needed to get done. Seperately, they were cold, and neither of them could think of the proper thing to do next. When she was done, Paige joined Kurt in the kitchen.
They met eyes as she walked through the kitchen doorway. They smiled at each other, but remained silent. Their wet and heavy clothes were sticking to them. Paige was a busy-body, as she took items out of her pantry. She started a pot of water on the stove, for tea or hot chocolate. She just couldn't decide which one to offer Kurt. "I'm starting water for something hot to drink, okay?" she said. "Okay," he replied. He watched in silence, in awe, at her quick moves. She turned on the oven then grabbed a large bowl from the top cabinet shelf. She opened containers of flour, sugar, oil, etc., got some eggs from the fridge and started mixing all of the ingredients in the bowl. Kurt smirked, as he quickly realized that she was making cookies. "Can I help?" he asked, wondering why she was doing what she was doing. "Sure," she replied. She slid the bowl to him, then asked him to continue stirring the dough. She got a cookie sheet from the lower cabinet, placed it on the counter, then announced what she was doing as she ran to the fireplace to check on the fire.

Kurt stirred, not knowing what to do next. He wondered, "Perhaps I should ask her to take me home? Perhaps I should walk home? I need to get out of these clothes, but I don't have anything to change into." Just then Paige came back into the kitchen. She asked Kurt to help her put the dough on the cookie sheet. They worked side-by-side, getting that task finished. Then Paige turned to him and said, "I'll let you take a shower and I will wash and dry your clothes, on one condition." Kurt was taken aback, smirked at her and replied, "Okay..." "I'll put the cookies in the oven, you can get undressed in the bathroom. There's a large bathrobe and dry towels in there..." She pointed in the direction of the bathroom. "Just put your clothes on the top of the washer."

Without another word, Kurt went into the bathroom. He felt compelled to do as she said. Both of them were running on adrenaline, just to stay warm, but equally they were not sure of what to do. Paige was in a mothering state-of-mind, but she also felt that she had no choice but to help him. Despite knowing now who he was and how much he had contributed to changing her life, she had to be a good samaritan. Once she heard that he was in the shower, she went to her bedroom, stripped and put on dry comfy clothes. She entered the bathroom and started the washer. "I'm doing the laundry now. It shouldn't interfere with your shower." "Thanks, Paige," he replied.

Paige stood in front of the washer. With a blank stare on her face, she didn't move for a few minutes. As she listened to Kurt in the shower, her mind wandered to a moment with her husband, who was showering after work one day. She smiled as she reminisced about hearing him hum to himself. She used to sit on the closed commode and talk with her husband, about his day, about the kids...as dinner would be in the oven. This odd moment with Kurt, in her shower, provoked a memory in her that was unwelcomed. For a split second, she wanted to get into the shower with Kurt...

Kurt was the reason why she was where she was, at least that was what her mind was telling her. She didn't completely blame him. She never forgave herself, either. She wondered why they were brought together that day, and why things had unfolded as they had. The sounding of her oven timer brought her out of her daze. She hurried back to the kitchen to turn it off, and to tend to the freshly baked cookies.

Kurt peeked out of the shower, getting a glimpse of Paige's back. He had no idea that she had been in the bathroom with him. She also never closed the door. Kurt had a moment of hesitation. He finished up, dried off while still in the shower, then stepped out with the towel wrapped around his waist.

Paige walked back into the bathroom, then quickly turned her back to Kurt. "Oh my god, I'm so sorry. I think the clothes are done. Put them in the dryer please." Paige quickly returned to the kitchen. She stood at the stove, taking the cookies off of the cookie sheet, and placing them on a plate. She smirked at the thought of Kurt's half-naked body. Paige almost let out a giggle at the thought of seeing his very fit chest and how he seemed to blush for a moment, but she recovered when the thought of her husband popped into her mind.

Paige heard Kurt start the dryer, then heard him enter the kitchen. She hesistantly turned around. He was mostly dressed, in her fluffy white robe. "I'm glad this fit me, otherwise this may have been too embarrassing." He walked a bit closer to Paige. "The cookies smell good." Paige smiled at him and told him that he looked fine, that she was glad that it fit him, too, and that he could help himself to the cookies. She placed the plate of cookies to

the left of the stove, then opened the oven door to help
warm the room.
"Both fires are going. We can sit in the living room if you
want. It should be warmer there," she said. "That sounds
great," he replied. Paige grabbed 2 cookies and headed for
the sunken living room. Kurt followed behind her, placing
one entire cookie in his mouth and grabbing two more
cookies.

Paige sat on the floor at the hearth of the fireplace and
placed a comforter around her shoulders. She had already
made hot chocolate for the both of them. She motioned for
Kurt to help himself. He joined her on the floor, with his
back against the couch, after picking up the mug of cocoa
from the end table.
They sat in silence, watching the embers glow and dance.
The fire crackled, they sipped their drinks slowly. They
thought, seperately, that it was odd that they would meet
each other that day. But they were also very grateful to
have survived what they had, up 'til then.
"How can I tell her how sorry I am, for what I had done?"
he wondered.
"How can I tell him that I have forgiven him?" she
wondered.

Paige enjoyed that time of sitting silently in front of the
fire. She cupped her mug with both hands, as she
reminisced about many moments with Jordan, at their
home, in front of their fireplace. Why was she feeling
relaxed, safe and comfortable, with Kurt there? She tried to
keep her thoughts on Jordan, but it was very difficult,
because she could smell Kurt. She could hear Kurt
slurping his hot chocolate. Their silence became awkward.
Each of them thought that they should say something, but
they weren't sure of what to say first. So they said nothing.

As time went slowly by, they got very tired. It was
inevitable that the warming fire would send them into
slumber. Just before Paige was about to doze off
completely, she reached for a pillow from the couch and
plopped it onto the floor. She sank into a nesting position
right in front of the fire, curled up into a ball and proceeded
to fall asleep.
Kurt's eyes were heavy as he watched her fall asleep. He,
too, became tired enough, comfortable enough, to fall
asleep as well. Still in a sitting position, he reached behind
him on the couch for a blanket and a pillow. He placed the
pillow on the floor, next to Paige's head, curled up near
her...closed his eyes, listened to her purring, and fell asleep.

While in deep slumber, Paige dreamed of her children.
They were playing in the backyard, along with Jordan,
throwing water balloons at each other. This made Paige
giggle, as she watched from her chair on the covered patio.
Paige giggled out loud, in her sleep, and for a passing
moment, Kurt heard her. He smiled, but never awoke.
In Paige's dream state, the scene quickly changed to a
moment that she was at home. The doorbell rang and she
answered the door. Two police officers were on her porch
with a look of pure sorrow. She started crying, in her deep
slumber, for she already knew what they were about to tell
her. She had relived that moment many nights, and in
many of her nightmares. She prayed many days for it to
stop. Her crying turned into audible sobs, in her dream.
But somehow, her sobs seeped out of her mind and into the
her living room.

Kurt woke to the sounds of her sorrows. He sat up, and
realized that she was still asleep. Paige was rocking in her
curled up position. Kurt was not sure of how to help her.
He got up, poked the dying fire and coaxed it into a roar.
He sat on the hearth and quietly watched Paige, as she

sobbed and rocked. He only hoped that what he was about
to do, would be welcomed and acceptable. Kurt knew that
sometimes his common sense was not so common. He also
wondered if he was awake or asleep.
He felt quite foggy. As he looked around the room, it
seemed to have filled up with smoke. Kurt got up, went to
the bathroom, got his clothes from the dryer and changed
back into his dungarees. Making his way through the
kitchen and back to the living room, he felt a sense of
urgency. There was smoke surrounding him, but he thought
it was odd that there was no smell from the fire. "Where
is the smoke coming from? The fire seems to be
contained in the fireplace," he thought.

As he got further into the living room, he could not see any
of the furniture in front of him. He could not even see his
own hands that he placed in front of him. "Oh my god," he
thought. "What is going on? I must still be asleep," he said
aloud. Kurt was almost completely blinded, as he felt
around for the couch and coffee table. He could not find
them.
The smoke lifted as he walked slowly toward where he
thought Paige lay. Kurt stopped in his tracks, as he saw
two small children emerge from the haze. These two
children were Paige's children. Kurt not only recognized
them, but had memorized their faces. Remorse filled his
soul at that very moment and he fell to his knees. He
covered his face and sobbed. They approached him, put
their hands on his shoulders and head, and together they
whispered, "It's okay. It's all forgiven. Mom is going to
need you now, more than ever." Sarah spoke softly, "Kurt,
mom is very sad, but we want her to be happy. We want
her to remember the fun times, not the sad ones." Dean
added, "We are with dad, so we will always be safe and
sound."

Kurt looked up. His surroundings had changed from the
comfort and warmth of Paige's living room, to dark and
foggy woods. He looked around and there were swaying
trees everywhere. He could smell the welcoming scent of
pines. Out from the fog, Jordan appeared. Kurt gasped.
Jordan placed his hands on his children's shoulders and lead
them backwards into the darkness. The children smiled at
Kurt, one last time. Kurt, still on his knees, looked in
amazement, not speaking a word. Jordan reappeared and
offered his hand to Kurt. Kurt put his hand in Jordan's
hand, and Jordan helped Kurt to his feet. In Kurt's eyes,
Jordan's appearance was perfect, with a simple light behind
him.
Jordon spoke, "Kurt, I will always love Paige, but she
needs you now. We know that you fell asleep. We know it
really wasn't your fault. We have forgiven you, and now it
is time for you to forgive yourself. I want you to take care
of My Love. Will you take care of her? Will you take care
of Paige?" Kurt's sobbing was reduced to soft crying.
He responded with a soft voice, "Yes. Yes, I will take care
of her. But... Has she forgiven me?" "Yes, Kurt, she has."
Kurt put his head in his hands and started crying again.
Jordan put a hand on Kurt's shoulder. "It's going to be
okay. You are going to be fine. Go to her. She deserves
your love and attention. She is ready for you."

When Kurt looked up, Jordan was gone. The fog had
cleared. He was back in Paige's living room. He turned
toward the fireplace and there was Paige, still in the same
spot as she was before. He could hear her purring as she
slept. She looked so peaceful, he thought. He wondered
how much time had passed. He looked at the clock on the
mantel, and it was the same time, when Paige had fallen
asleep. He sat down next to her and outstretched his hands
to get them warm from the fire. Paige reached up and put
her hand in his. He looked down at her. Her face was so

beautiful to him, the fire was softly and brilliantly dancing in her green eyes. "Lay with me, please," she whispered. "You make me feel safe." As Kurt curled up next to her, he wrapped his strong arms around her. He pulled her closer to him, and whispered, "You are safe. I am here for you. I will always take care of you, My Love."
Paige closed her eyes and sighed. His deep voice comforted her back into slumber. In her mind's eye, she saw Jordan, Dean and Sarah smile at her, as they disappeared into a foggy forest. Out from behind her, Kurt emerged from the fog. He wrapped his arms around her. She smiled back at them and waved goodbye. She knew at that moment, that she was safe and sound in her new Love's arms. She knew her children were safe with Jordan. She knew that it was okay to move on.

NIGHT SOUNDS
(Late September, 2016)

Has that cricket always been chirping?
She didn't remember hearing him earlier in this night.
Her nighttime tea ritual must've helped because she just didn't remember falling asleep.
Perhaps she didn't fight so hard this time, as this time hasn't been any different than the previous seven nights.
It's almost always at night.

The crying came out of nowhere. Or is it from somewhere? It's slightly hidden in the ripples and recesses of her impacted brain, and with a methaphoric "snap," it comes to the surface.
She feels her face crinkle, her lips start to quiver, her hands cover her mouth, then her eyes, and right back to her

mouth, as she does her grandest to muffle the sounds of the heartache that continued to show up.

"I must be quiet."

There's no one to call, to cry to, to vent to, to scream at, as her suffering must go, unnoticed, for it's unwarranted, it's unfair of her, to waste other's times, for they've heard it all before. From this person's mouth, to their ears, and as always, they are as tired of it, as she is, if not more so.

"Who can I tell?...that another time has come where I suffer alone, I cry a lot, I ache for his company, I ache for his laugh, his smile. I'm never enough.
I'm never going to be enough."

His words of...
"I view you as my meal ticket,"
"This is the summer of you," and
"I'm not in love with you,"
should crush her beyond recognition...should make her facade look shattered, as shattered as her heart is...
His words should have burned her, from the outside in and the inside out, ripping her skin from its bones, leaving her in a pile of thick water and dust.
It should turn her skin grey, with cloudy eyes, dark circles, unglittered skin, with nails unsharp, blemished heels, dull hair and cracked lips.
It should burn through her blackening heart
and blackening soul.

But, alas, No! Paint as paint can be done, with brushes, coiffes, glosses, sprays, more paint and polish...and a prayer on its way for that day. She realized again, that it's truly hard to put mascara on ocean waves of watered eyes...

Red, black and blue eyes, staring at the mirrored corpse
before her.

"I'm dying...again"...and she prays that she doesn't recover.

"I want to melt into the cracks of my floor, into the crevices
of my apartment, into the bumps and unsmoothed textures
of my plastered walls, and melt into the cold grout of the
ancient tile that lines my bathroom floor."
As she would melt, she'd allow herself to die, an unpublic
slow death, as she rightly deserved.
...the fool that she is, the fool that she's always been, as she
freely admits her mistakes of letting him touch her already
scared, scarred and bruised heart...again.

Never will she give in again to the idea of love everlasting,
never will she give into the idea of a friendship of a former
lover, never will she find reciprocal love, because she knew
at that moment, it was never meant for her.
She'll never have it, she never deserved it. Never.

She welcomed the cold hard tile, touching her naked warm
body, after the shower that she forced herself to take...as
she slumped to the floor, crying, wailing, asking
why, why, why?...
Knowing full-well why: Need, Want, Lust, Friendship,
Desire, Love, Happiness, Contentment, Safety, Comfort,
Family...and the hopes of never having to wander, wonder,
worry or look, ever again.
Her future scared her.
Not much of a future, she tells herself.

At that moment, her lifetime dreams died a horrible, but
deserved death. No one...to be around to console her and
hug her and rock her to sleep and weep, when her father
passes...much like the moments, the days and the months

that she dredged in, all alone, when her mother died long
ago. It was like yesterday.
The memory dashed forward, then the loneliness, the
heartache, the knowledge of facing that impending time
alone, again, had become unbearable.

"No one..."

After the shivering began and the waters subsided a bit, the
corpse reached up and inside the confines of the bathroom
cabinetry, finding the sharp object she desired... She began
chopping, cutting with fervor, hacking away the curls and
waves, hacking away at her beautiful long auburn mane
which had taken many a-day to grow.
She did so, allowing the regret to surface,
but she could not stop.
Left with chopped bits, with auburn flowing to the floor, an
uneven mane surfaced, and the wailing persisted. She
clenched her fists, pounded her fists into her temples, held
them there for a moment, whereas to keep her head
from exploding.
With limited strength, she pulled the remainder of her once
beautiful waves from her scalp, silently screaming, then
again, she slumped to the floor, and she temporarily
melted...

The wailing subsided.
Sobbing, she crawled to her desk, found her paper and
digital daily writings and journals, then ripped them to
shreds, and crushed them with a nearby boot heel...and
promised "never again."
Sobbing, she crawled to her bed, and with what little
strength she had left, she pulled herself into it, covered
herself up, covering her bruised and battered and bleeding
bald head. Her tears, and blood, soaked her pillowcase,

soaked through her pillow and mattress, and pooled onto
the floor beneath her bed.

The blood and tears seeped into the floorboards, down
through the concrete, into the dirt and dust, and flowed
into, and in between, the jagged plates of the earth.

As her tears began to slow and her thoughts began to quiet,
she heard the chirp of the cricket in her window sill.

As she rocked back and forth, she felt her lover's arms
around her, she felt his warm breath on her neck, she
continued to melt...

She was aware that she was voluntarily dying, just as she
wanted, just as she deserved. Along with her naïve,
unnecessary, childish dreams, she gave up, she gave in, to
Death.

The cricket's rhythmic song lulled her to sleep, and she
wondered, "Has that cricket always been singing?"

IN SEARCH OF THE OLD WORLD

(This is a story I wrote on October 17th, 1979, in a Creative
Writing class. In red ink, at the top of the page, my teacher
wrote: "Very good 25/25." I have rewritten it, just as I had
written it back then, except I added a bit of necessary
punctuation, etc., so it could be understood. Laugh if you
must...but also enjoy it)

"The Environmental Wars" had been over for 20 years now
and the damage that the "Participants" had done was
enormous.
No one lived on the surface since the last invention: a
machine to capture air. There were no plants, no animals,
no mountains. The Earth was like one huge deserted
ghost town.
Inventions before, were bombs to destroy life, movement of
mountains, depositing of garbage in oceans, draining of
rivers, and using up all natural resources.
Individual citizen organizations overthrew the government
and took over the world by inventions to gain power.
Before the government was completely overthrown, it set
up jobs for future living by starting a plan for a union to
begin building underwater and underground cities. By
doing so, they invented artificial suns, trees, houses,
markets, courts, railways. The building and finishing of
this, because of machine technology and computers, took
only 19 ½ years. The ending point was estimated at 25
years, but advanced science proved itself well.

It is the year 5352.7 and Victoria P-475 and Ike 26-NK are
together at Kegans Hall, a Recreation area at the North of
Earth.
Like everyone, they wear brown boots, white slacks and a
pleated shirt, and gold identification neckbands.

They sit at the fountain located at 75 degrees-25 degrees of the center. They are talking about The Exam that every school person takes. If there is a five-year old and a 16-year old (like Victoria and Ike) taking the test, and they both get 100%, the five-year old will not have to go on to school, and neither will the 16-year old.
Forty percent of the people who passed were eighteen, and sixty percent were younger than 18. One third of that sixty percent were six years old and younger.
The young students who passed were either to work or rest. There wasn't any college.

"What do you think you got on The Exam?" Ike asked.
"I think I got an "A." How about you?"
"Maybe a "B." I can't wait until the results to come back in five months. Can you?"
"No. I wish it didn't have to take that long," Victoria responded. "That's not what used to happen when great-grandpa was our age. He used to get it the next day."
"You can't go by that. It takes five months because all the people 18 and under of the Earth takes The Exam all at once."
"I know. I just want it to be like great-grandpa's world," Victoria replied.
"You know when the Wars were on, that some buildings were destroyed, including City Halls and Libraries. That means we have NO proof of how it was before, except for old people's memories and fantasies," Ike stated.
By that statement, Victoria started to remember stories about Divers of the Oceans, Walkers of Parks and Surface Cities, Flyers of Air and Space, and Soakers of the Sun. Those stories were told by her 501-year old great-grandpa, when all the family was together twelve years earlier. She sighed as she wondered if they were tales or reality. Her attention was drawn back to Ike as he asked if she wanted to go to the Ocean View. He said he would pay for both of

their ways, and she agreed. She said she would pay their
way next time.
Ike had made reservations ahead of time, to go to the Ocean
View. They were lucky to get to go.

"Ocean View: Where everybody goes to dream," the
advertisement stated on monitors everywhere.

Ocean View is the last remaining strip of a square mile
stretch of ocean. The Aqua Cars are spread all over the
ocean and run past the mile of water in all directions. What
fills the rest of where the ocean would be, is trash, garbage
of all kinds (one of the inventions of the Wars and its
aftermath).
People would pay $100 dollars apiece to see this vast
spread of ocean water, seaweed, sand and coral, but no fish.
All the animals were wiped out in the Wars.
They were off! They rode through the Rock Cars to Ocean
View. It only took them four hours to get from where they
lived, what Surface People used to call Greenland, to the
middle of the Pacific, which was now called Pahifico.
When they arrived, they walked on the Side-Ways for
about a mile, as the markers had indicated, until they
reached the main view screen. They set their eyes on the
most beautiful sight that they had ever seen before. As far
as they could see, it was all ocean, a green and blue world.
Many generations before them had lived on the surface and
could swim the oceans, breathe "free" air, watch nature
work. Victoria decided now that the stories her great-
grandpa had told her MUST be true. He couldn't have
made it up.
She mumbled to herself, "Would I be able to know what it's
like on the surface?"
Ike interrupted her, "Let's go. The guards will be coming
soon and they will chase us away. Our five minutes are
almost up."

They walked to the Aqua Cars, rode until they got to the
Rock Cars, and rode again back to the Recreation area.
Victoria timidly stated, "I'm gonna see the surface."
"What?" Ike asked. "Nothing, nothing. I will see you
tomorrow. Bye."

After each one went to their separate rooms, the Seven foot
clock struck 4:00pm. Victoria settled in, after a few
minutes of preparing for bed. She lay there, with her eyes
wide open, as she looked over her entire room, noticing all
of her belongings.
Over to the right of the dorm was her Personal Viewer for
school, which she used to take The Exam. To her extreme
right were her photos of her family; her great-grandparents
and their kids, her grandparents and their kids, her parents
and her deceased brother Cary M-7FQ. How she missed
them so. When they were taken away to the South of
Earth, to level out the population, she was only four years
old.
To her extreme left was the entertainment center where she
sat and listened to historical and modern music. The
entertainment center's computers had recorded all of the
music from yesteryears, and that was all they had left to
remind them of those times.
She loved to listen to the different types of music and guess
what the people were like, when the music was produced
and popular.
To her left as well, was the Exchanger, as her teacher
stated, it was a typical 54th Century device. One would step
in and the computerized hands would dress and undress its
user.
Victoria got up, went over to her entertainment center and
flipped the switch. She sat down and pushed the
coordinates: 20th Century, Popular Ballad G-O. The center
started playing "Born Free." When the song was over,
Victoria got up and when she got to her bed, the center

finished by stating in a deep, manly voice: "All right, slick chicks and cool dudes, that was the fantastically beautiful song "Born Free," and we are all free, ain't we?" Then a sound of a click, the center turning itsefl off.
"That does not compute," the center came back on automatically. The center's computers were confused and Victoria was puzzled as well. "Hmmm," she mumbled. She slowly crawled into bed and fell asleep as soon as her head hit the pillow.

The next day, Ike and Victoria unitentionally ran into each other at the Information and Locations Building in Wilton - Z Court.
"What are you doing here?" Victoria asked.
Ike responded, "Didn't you ask me to come here?"
"No," she snapped back.
"I don't know then. I think I just came because I thought to..."
Victoria asked, "It just popped into your head?"
"Yeah. Why are you here?" Ike asked.
"To get information and locations."
"About what?" Ike asked.
Victoria hesitated with her answer, "W-Where guards and policemen are gonna be at, what locations and when."
Ike looked puzzled, "Why?"
Victoria whispered, "So...I can catch them off-guard and make it to the Personal Shafts, to get to the surface."
"You can't go to the surface!" Ike exclaimed. "You'll be shot on sight, and besides, what's up there for you?"
"Freedom," Victoria firmly stated.
Ike paused for a moment, then emphasized in a whisper, "I'll help. I'm coming, too."
"Great," Victoria replied.
They entered the building and carefully studied the directions.

"At 3:10pm, which is in about an hour and a half, the guards will be switching at Quadrant 1160. That's the one we will need. We'll make our way there, okay?" Victoria instructed. "Right," Ike agreed.

"Let's go pick up grandpa now and we'll tell him our plan." Ike asked, "Why him?"

"He'll have to tell us what everything is, when we get on the surface," Victoria replied.

"But the surface is bound to be rubble, you know that," Ike stated.

"Don't be too sure. Why do you think they have caves and shafts?" she asked.

"For the people to get below when the Wars were going on."

Victoria stated, as a matter of fact, "Yeah, but they would have closed them up if they knew we'll never return to the surface. I just know they've been doing something up there."

"How do you know that?" asked Ike.

"I just have a feeling. Like when you had a feeling to meet me here." Vicoria replied.

"Aha. Come on, let's go!" Ike exclaimed.

They took off to Grandpa Chester's dorm and told him of their plan. He readily agreed and helped them prepare for their journey.

"It's ten minutes until 3 o'clock," Victoria whispered.

"Let's look around and remember the UnderWorld. These few minutes are going to be long ones."

She was right. The fifteen minutes they spent were like fifteen hours.

Finally, it was time to go and they sneaked over to the fence. The lively old man climbed over first, then Victoria, then Ike. They crouched low and hurried over the tall brick wall, where the Steps lead to the Surface.

In the Monitoring Room: "Hey, Charlie, it's 3:10pm. Any disturbances?"
"No. How long until your shift is over?"
"Oh, around twelve o'clock."
Two of the guards walked outside toward the fleet of jeeps. Just then, they heard Victoria yell, "Now!" The three escapees scrambled toward the Steps. Their legs were sore from their trek, but they managed to climb.

Then sirens shrieked, "Rrrrr."
Over the PA system: "People escaping into the Shafts! Guards, get them!"

"Four hundred feet!" Victoria yelled in her mind. "That's eight hundred steps!"
"Eight hundred steps to climb," Ike wondered, "That would be 400 steps if I hit two at a time..." "If I take four at a time," Chester thought, "I'd only hit 200 steps."

They leaped, ran, jumped, skipped and stomped on the stairs. Sweat was dripping down their backs and faces... Ike, who was second in the race, wondered aloud at times, "Is this really worth it?" Victoria replied, every time, "Yes!"
The guards were so close behind them, that Victoria thought she felt their hot breaths on her neck. They were falling behind very fast. "I can see the light up ahead!" Chester screamed. "Hurry!" Ike yelled. "I don't think I can make it!" yelled Victoria. "You can, Victoria. You can't give up," Chester and Ike yelled in unison. Victoria was breathing heavily and her heart felt as if it were about to burst.

Ike reached down, grabbed her wrist, and pulled her up to him. They walked the remaining steps. The guards seemed to retreat. Chester placed his hands on the lid of the shaft, closed his eyes and pushed on it until it was wide open. He walked up and jumped onto a dirt road. Victoria and Ike stared up at the blue sky in amazement. They squinted and called out to Chester, "Grandpa? Gramps?"

They heard him exclaim, "Yaaaa-hoooo!"
"Ya-hoo?"
"Come on up, kids. It's bea-u-ti-ful!"

Ike pushed Victoria up and then climbed out himself. They held their hands over their eyes for a bit until they got used to the light. They looked around awestruck.
There were small houses covered with hay, fields of green and gold, fences, barns, trees, horses, cows, children and adults...all working and playing in the surrounding fields. All of them recognized what they were seeing, from the picture books at school.
"This is what has been going on," Chester informed them. "What they taught you about the Surface was all lies."
"But why?" asked Ike.
"The Participants were going to see if they could correct what they did wrong twenty years ago. The Surface was deserted for a while, but the people you see now were part of the Program that The Participants started. They wanted to have a new start.
"Is it like this throughout the world?" Ike asked.
"Yes."
"When were we to find out?"
"Not for a long time. And this is not soon enough either," Chester replied.
Victoria and Ike smiled broadly when the people of the village came up to them and said, "Hello. From the UnderGround?"
"Yes," The exhausted three replied. "We are very pleased to meet you. Very much."

It was the beginning of a new life, a new world, for the
three of them. Victoria's mind was racing, as she thought
of ways to get the word out, that there was life on the
Surface. There was life, alright. New people to her, new
things to see, touch, smell and she had a long list in her
head, of where to start first...

THE MYSTERY OF ST. ASTAIN
(I had written this story from a dream that I had had,
around the age of ten. I wrote the story many years later.
Even to this day, when I read it, it makes me laugh a bit. It
is quite cute and I hope that you find it just as cute)

Dreams can baffle any person, especially when everything
about them seems so real, even if they're little things. I
want to relate to you a story about my experience of that
nature.

I jumped out of a big brass bed, with an unusual colored
quilt on it. I had heard someone scream. I looked all over
the bedroom, which I had never seen before. It had a
nineteenth century dresser, with a huge round mirror on the
top. The curtains were made of ruffled blue silk, and there
were little statuettes of men that I remembered seeing in
horror films. There were panels in the wall, that, with the
slightest touch, creaked. I approached the mahogany door,
and grasped the glass doorknob. It was cold. The door
squeaked as I slowly opened it.

I saw a staircase that went spiraling downward, and one
that went straight upward. I heard voices downstairs, and I
went toward them. The first stair that I stepped on creaked

really loud. The voices stopped, feet scrambled, then I
heard a crash, as if someone had knocked over a glass vase
or glass figure. Then I heard nothing. I continued down,
and as I got to the last step, my eyes opened really wide.
My mouth opened even wider.

Glass windows, glass chairs, glass tables, clocks and even
the floor looked like glass. I walked across the floor,
whirled around, and called out, "Hello?" All I heard was
the echo bouncing off of the walls and fading away.
I walked into the room that had a very tall entrance. It must
have been a ballroom. The floor was checkered black and
white. There were several small windows all around. I
immediately noticed the two see-through doors that led to
the balcony. I could see the tall redwood trees in the
background.

I approached the doors, swung them open and stepped onto
the terrace. I sniffed the morning air and it was heavenly.
I peered over and saw the white patio chairs out on the
lawn, which was like a plush green carpet. I saw below,
rolling valleys and beyond them were craggy mountains. I
finally decided to explore this floor first, then go back
upstairs, check on the attic next, and then go down to the
basement. Lastly, I would check the grounds on which this
amazing and creepy house stood.

I went into the kitchen which looked like one from the
Middle Ages, with an old-fashioned stove and cupboards.
From a bowl on the table, I chose a large apple and put it in
my pocket to eat later. My search of the rooms downstairs
took about an hour, I supposed, then I proceeded to the
second floor. Still, I ran into no one...

The first bedroom that I entered was better decorated than
the one in which I had awoken. It must have been a man's

room, because there were bottle of after-shave on the
dresser, a man's wrist watch and a pair of trousers hanging
over a chair. I went to the next bedroom door, which was
closed. I turned the doorknob and pushed, but it would not
open. As I was about to turn and leave, I heard someone or
something inside. I decided to try to ignore it and my
conscience let me. I started to go downstairs, but I changed
my mind and headed for what I assumed was the door to
the attic.

Just then I heard a loud, shrill scream from above.
"Someone's in the attic," I said to myself. I opened the
door, and rushed up the stairs. Nothing. All it was, was an
insulated attic, with various rickety and rudimentary wares.
Another scream came, and a loud growl, but that time if
was from somewhere below. I ran from the attic, down the
long, narrow hall and down the spiral stairs, through the
dining room, into the kitchen, and to the door which I
believed would lead me to the basement. I opened it.

Darkness. I felt for the light switch, turned it on and crept
slowly down the steps and onto the bare floor. Upon my
descent, I ran into spider webs and cob webs, that I had to
constantly brush from my face. I heard a growl behind me!
I flew around and screamed as loud as I could.
IT WAS A WEREWOLF!

A shot rang out. The creature ran around a corner and
disappeared. Quickly, I ran back up the steps, into the
kitchen, then into the living room. Suddenly someone
tapped on my left shoulder and I spun around. There was a
man of about sixty-fice and ugly, too. His trousers, shirt,
jacket, shoes and cape, were all black. I could see
gleaming white fangs as he smiled and said in a
distinguished accent, "Sit down, please."

We both sat down and I asked him where we were.
"We are on an uncharted island in the middle of some
unknown ocean, where no one comes to visit, except for the
ones that I choose." He said in a deeper, move moving
voice, that some people come but few ever get to leave. I
thought he was trying to scare me, and it worked. I
nervously sat back in the chair and said, "Go on..."
He proceeded to tell me that the house was built in 1798.
The furniture and accessories were brought in month by
month, year by year. He preferred to call it his castle.
The castle's name was St. Astain.

"The people who left from the island soon went crazy and
were put in asylums," he contined, "No one believed their
stories. The ones who didn't leave, as I mentioned, were
put to work. Some cooporated, but the ones who did not,
were put in the dungeon below the basement." He told me
that his name was Julian and the creature's name was
Magnus.
"Magnus has been with me for forty-five years now. He
prefers to wear my clothing when he is in his true form and
he despises women. I advise you to keep away from him
and don't be caught alone in the same room with him, or
he'll dig his claws into your lovely neck. Do you
understand me?"
"Of course," I said nervously. "Where is the girl who
screamed?"
"It's a slave girl who refused to work."
"How did she get here?"
"She and her newlywed husband, Bernard, were on a
honeymoon yacht trip a couple of months ago. Magnus
saw them on our radar and we decided to haul them in. It
was a frightening experience for them, and of course, for all
of the other visitors as well. You, too, would be frightened
if the ocean sucked you up in a whirlpool for no reason at
all. We decided to bring them in as workers. Naturally,

being sensible, the man agreed, but Gail didn't want to
work. We had to punish her. Bernard tried to interfere, so
we sent him back to the States. We knew that nobody
would believe anything he had to say."
"What are you going to do with her?"
"I put her in the dungeon with her hands and feet
chained to the wall."
"How horrible!" I exclaimed, in disgust.
"Why are you telling me all of this?"
"Because you will never get a chance to repeat it," he
snapped.

As I listened for the next ten minutes, I had realied that I
could not move. I was entranced by his words. I was
captured by his evil spell. As the clock chimed nine
o'clock, he told me that it was time for his rest. He told me
to go back to my bedroom and I fought to comply, but
something overtook me and I went upstairs to the bedroom
in which I had awoken. I slipped under the quilt, fluffed
the pillow, then sat upright in the bed. "This has got to be a
dream," I said aloud. "All these weird rooms and the
unexplained noises...loud screams and the feeling that
someone is staring at me through the portraits and panels.
Terribly spooky. Why am I sitting here?"
I laid down, slid further into the bed, rolled over onto my
side, and in spite of my troubled thoughts, I uncontrollably
fell asleep.

I was awakened by a strange noise. I looked across the
room. It was only the tree branches rubbing against the
window, due to the strong winds. When I got up, I saw that
I was in a nightgown, so I got dressed in my clothes and
went to the spiral stairs. As before, I heard voices down
below. It was Julian talking to someone.

I heard him say, "....and we're going to have to kill them both tomorrow...the one upstairs and the one in the dungeon."

I was horribly frightened. He was going to kill us for no reason at all! I knew I had to get that girl from downstairs, and fast.
But I knew that I would have to wail until they went back to bed. I decided that now was an excellent time to investigate the locked room. I quietly left my room...
I carefully turned the knob and pushed. It was unlocked. Entering, I saw all kinds of modern technological equipment; revolutionized computers, sound sensory devices, calculators, radar screens, several camera monitors, data processors, and many other machines that I did not recognize.

After examing them, I walked to the console in the center of the room.
On it were some files marked: Top Secret.
I looked inside.
It was information and photos of everyone who had ever come to the island, including photos of me and information about me! Near the files, lay a .22 caliber gun. This I picked up and slipped into my pocket.

Some time had passed, as I examined all around me, then I returned to the stairway. Hearing nothing, I assumed that they were asleep and made my way down to the dungeon. I went into the cold, dimly lit room and saw the girl stretched against the wall. She was very pretty, with long red hair, green eyes and the most frightened look on her face.
"Don't be afraid," I said, "I'm going to help you." The chains were not very big, so I used the gun to shoot them loose. As she rubbed her wrists and ankles, she thanked me and asked who I was and what I was doing there.

"I don't know how I got here," I replied, "but I am going to save our necks. Those people are going to kill us, so we've got to leave now!" We ran up the stairs to the basement level, then on up to the kitchen, out the back door, and then around the front of the house. Great luck! There was a boat dock with a rowboat tied to it. We ran to it, jumped in and cast off.

We rowed until we were exhausted. The waves rocked the boat and came over the side, drenching us with icy waters. It seemed as if we were doomed when Gail pointed to a small grey object in the distance. As it slowly came nearer, we could see it was the Coast Guard. Both of us screamed and waved until they saw us and brought us on board. When we were warm and dry, we told them our story. They believed us!!

A few minutes later, Gail's husband Bernard appeared and they wept as they were reunited. I watched and cried as they never stopped hugging each other.
When were repeated our story to the authorities, once we were ashore, preparations were made to return to the island and arrest the men. Of course, Gail, Bernard and I insisted on going along to help recover all of the files, camera equipment, etc., and help with saving many others who were still trapped there.

Once we approached the island, along with many of the Coast Guard personnel, we came to the dock, jumped out and ran to the castle. Each of us scattered in different directions, entering different doorways to get inside. As I crept into the kitchen, I hesitantly began to climb the stairs. When I reached the top, I could see that there was a light coming from underneath the door of the computer room. I tiptoed towards the door, cautiously opened it and found that the room was unoccupied. Quickly, I went to the console, opened all of the drawers and found the files that I wanted. I took them, turned on my heels and got out of that room as fast as I could. Just as I reached the stairs, I was grabbed by someone, spun around, and shook very hard. "Honey, it's time to get up and get ready for school." My mother was shaking me awake.

I sat up and said, shockingly, "I'm in my own room."
"Of course," Mom said. "Now, get up, get dressed for school, and please pick up your dirty clothes off of the floor and put them in the hamper."
After I got dressed, I grabbed up the clothes that I had worn the day before. An apple fell out and rolled across the floor. "But it was a dream!" I yelled. "It must have been."
"I will just try to forget the whole thing," I thought.
"But can I?"

MICHELLE
(I met Michelle in 2008...)

Michelle worked at the Breads and Baskets Bakery in her hometown. It was a small bakery servicing a diverse population. She provided great customer service to customers from all walks of life. She loved her job and planned to own her own bakery someday.
From the time this one male customer walked into the bakery, Michelle had experienced a bit of anxiety. There was something about that man that gave her chills up her spine. His gaze seemed to go right through her and he seemed to always be staring at her. Because of his ethnic background, he had an accent that made it hard for Michelle to understand him. That seemed to intensify her anxiety. She would sweat a lot, her heart would race, and

she was not able to have a clear thought every time he came around.

Michelle consulted the internet and went to the library for some answers on her level of anxiety. She began to feel quite isolated. Her co-workers did not seem to acknowledge her reactions and she noticed that they did not have the same reactions when seeing that one particular customer. She read that anxiety was a reaction to stress (real or imagined), possibly anger, and that it was a way of alerting someone to conflict, and may, in some ways, impair one's life. She did not like the way these things were affecting her, with lack of sleep, unclear thinking, sporadic eating and just trouble with day-to-day living. However, her anxiety would intensify when she would see that man outside of work; at the grocery store, the bank, etc. At times she would feel as if she was being followed. She felt threatened by this thought. She began to feel intense emotions and physical changes, like goose bumps and rising blood pressure.

She began to fear leaving her home. She would become forgetful of the time, and sometimes be late to work. She became irritable at work and sometimes could not concentrate. She had a hard time dealing with headaches and felt that she was taking too much medication to get rid of them.

She got angry with her co-workers and short-tempered with the customers. She began to avoid the customers and tell her co-workers to take over her position. She would remove herself from the service counter and take over for another worker in the back room. At times, the overwhelming fear, anger and helplessness would make her break down and cry. Most of the time the crying would be unprovoked.

Her co-workers finally gave her advice to seek counseling and consult the police about her concerns about her odd customer, although they did not feel threatened by him.

Michelle felt that at least talking to someone about her concerns would help. Upon advice from her doctor, she began to redirect her nervous energy into cleaning the house, journaling, doing the laundry, dusting, and reorganizing her limited belongings. She decided to do some Spring cleaning, getting rid of things that she no longer needed.

She was not in a position to quit her job or even to lose some much-needed hours. She was poor afterall. Her supervisor let her stay in the back, which helped her out a lot.

Michelle started meditating, doing yoga, listening to soothing music, and participated in art activities at home and at outside venues. She read articles on self-awareness, mood management and did her best to get down to the bottom of the source of her anxiety.

Upon her day of Spring cleaning, she found a box of photos from her childhood. In this box were photos from her old neighborhood...and in one particular photo, which was taken in front of her modest home in Indiana, was a man standing next to her parents and her two brothers. Her parents were long gone, and upon viewing this photo, Michelle began to sob.

Suddenly her anxiety had become clear. Her customer reminded her of the man in that photograph. The man in the photo was a dear friend of her family and was her dad's co-worker and also his best friend. Alex. He was a kind and sincere man, who had spent many days with her family, had been invited to all of their holiday meals and holiday parties, and he had been long forgotten by Michelle. He had been her confidante, spending time with her and family, at the backyard cookouts, helping out with their gardens of flowers, lettuce, onions, pumpkins and rhubarb. She remembered telling him many of her deepest and silly secrets, about her grade school crushes and crushes on bubblegum stars.

The memory of her parents was always with her, but why did she forget this wonderful man? Michelle was not sure. Michelle took a moment to relive the day that her parents and their friend, Alex, had died in a plane crash, when she was only eight years old. She sat quietly on the floor of her bedroom, closed her eyes and relived the moment. Each of them had kissed her forehead and the foreheads of each of her brothers. They said goodbye to them and the babysitter, and had gotten in their car and waved goodbye. That was the last time that she had seen all of them. She remembered the phone call that the babysitter had received and that she had collapsed to the floor, sobbing from the news. She had remembered the babysitter asking her brothers and her to sit down. She remembered the feel of the worn-down couch beneath her, as she gripped the edge of the cording on the cushion. She had watched the face of her babysitter as she struggled to tell them that her parents and Alex had died. She remembered that her family friend and confidante was gone forever. Besides her family, whom she loved dearly and would always remember, Alex was her first true best friend. His loss was so deep that she must have washed it away from her mind. She decided that she needed to change her attitude toward her customer and perhaps find the means to be more kind and turn around her anxiety to empathy and compassion. Michelle found peace in her newfound thoughts. Michelle found peace within herself.

HER LOVE STORY
(...from seventh grade...and, yeah, don't laugh too hard)

One summer evening, a long time ago,
There was a maiden named Lorallia.
Daily, she wore white, green and red gowns,
Which were her favorite colors.
She was very proud of her handmade attire.
She had red hair and a lovely face.
Everyone in the village had admired her floating walk.
She lived in the Middle Ages, when the nights were filled
With beauty and color, the days were filled with
song and dance.
The fields were filled with golden wheat and green grass,
The sky was filled with blue, white and grey colors,
And birds, of course.

Lorallia was sitting underneath her most favored tree
– the oak.
"Mister Oak," she called it.
Lorallia was in love with a man not much older than she.
His name was Anton.
He lived in a yellow cottage with brown trim
Not far from the small village.

What Lorallia did not know was that Anton had loved her
Just as much as Lorallia had loved him.
He didn't tell anyone because he thought
he was beneath her status.
One night, Anton met Lorallia in the "Valley of the Heart,"
Where lovers tell each other of their intentions.
Anton told Lorallia he loved her very much.
She told him the same.

Two years later, they announced to the village
That they were going to marry and have a lovely

Marriage ceremony near her favorite tree.
On that important day, Lorallia got into her great
Grammy's wedding gown.
It was white, trimmed with red velvet and red lace,
And it had a viel made of white lace.
The wedding was at six gongs of the bell,
Then it was time to get to the chapel.
Lorallie and Anton hurried into the small church,
Walked down the aisle and stopped
at the foot of the preacher.

Lorallia's mind drifted, as she dreamed
of daisies and posies,
Collecting them, keeping them and smelling them.
She could foresee having many children,
All of whom their mighty King would embrace.
The preacher said the final words,
then they scurried to their carriage.
All the people of the village waved goodbye,
Hoping and sobbing for their happiness.
They rode off down the fog-laden path...
Lorallia's dreams came true.
Everyone was happy including the King
And of course, they lived happily ever after.

TAYLOR SWIFT
(A <u>small</u> letter to you, since I saw you for the first time,
more than seven years ago)

To this lovely lady, I can't help but see grace
and creativity at its finest.
Many of your words continue to hit me hard,
like a cartoon anvil to my head.
I've wondered, "How can this young-un feel so much pain,
at such a young age, when it has taken me years of pain,
to acknowledge and pen <u>my</u> pain?"

Unbeknownst to me, your song "Teardrops On My Guitar"
would become the one song that makes me tear up every
time I hear it. For it was my first exposure to you...and
therefore, admiration of you and your ongoing efforts of
making a difference to many young girls.
This old gal still feels pangs and sorrows, as I seem to
suffer along with you.
...For not knowing the reasons behind the many cheatings
and lyings and betrayals that came shooting my way, that
keep me trapped inside my own thoughts
...of which I see and feel no escape.

"Teardrops" was the song, that started my downfall
awareness of my beau's desires for another. There was
something about that song that struck me, as I watched
your video and sobbed like a baby...in front of my beau of
three years, who in turn rolled his eyes at me.
He made mention of disliking you...out of jealousy of some
kind, I'm sure...and at that moment, and with many
moments afterwards, my heart opened up to the knowledge
of his cheating on me.

I wanted to remain blind and dumb. I tried to convince
myself that "what I didn't know, wouldn't kill me." But in
fact, Taylor, I did know. And it nearly killed me.
My gut was in an uproar, my head was always
pounding...although his demeanor was not clearly apparent
to my naked eyes. My gut was not talking to my head and
heart, my body was no longer in sync with itself. I was
more than uncomfortable, as I repeatedly told myself that
something was wrong, other than just my own health.
When confronted, he verbally reassured me of nothing,
otherwise...

He let me suffer, as he knew the cure to my own pain:
The truth.
Visitations to doctors didn't help. He let me suffer, for all
he had to do was tell me (the truth). He failed to do so, for
over ten months...as he was "doing her, while doing me."
Sorry for the TMI.
He finally came clean and clear with me...this chicken, over
the phone...admitting his guilt...on a holiday, no doubt...and
while he listened to me bawl...
I have never been more embarrassed...for he laughed at my
multiple sufferings...

He laughed at me, Taylor, during our converstion of his
breaking it off...and I have yet to recover since that
horrible, dreadful day. This man, whom I loved
wholeheartedly...whom I was to move in with...who
promised to take me to the hospital, the following month
for surgery...who promised to take care of me after said
surgery...and with whom had initially tried to break it off
via texting on Thanksgiving, of all holidays!

He laughed at me...

And so I pen.

And so I listen to "Teardrops" with many teardrops in my
eyes, that do not fall down on my guitar...but fall onto my
chest, my shirt...and sometimes onto the floor, where I
throw myself...bawling and balling up and wanting to bail
out...daily, and even still, metaphorically.

I have seen myself grow, as I watch you grow, into the
most interesting and talented woman that I don't know.
You have penned my sorrows.
You have penned my feelings.
I have admiration of you, as you have become the most
wonderful success to women.
Those of us who love your words and actions and
compassion, will continue to love the works that you do.
I would love to live up to the standards
that one like you possesses.
But only after I have cried my last teardrop.
12/15
Sincerely and with deep admiration,
JJP

IF SOMETHING HAPPENS TO ME TODAY

(Written one night, feeling a bit lonely and sad, and I
assume, feeling quite sorry for myself, too...late, 2013)

If something happens to me today, my brother has my
Will and knows my true wishes.
Give my non-perishable foods to charity.

My kids can do whatever they want with my belongings.
My suggestion is for them to look through everything, sell
everything that they think would be of value and split the
money, not that it would be much. I have been spending
some time getting rid of mostly everything, so when
something happens to me, they would have less to deal
with...

I have always hoped to be no burden to anyone.
They may need help with organizing whatever is left.
Dad, I hope you can help, when available.

I know this note is not legal, but it should be...

My brother knows who I would want to have a say in my
arrangements and he knows who should not have a
say...and who should not be present at my service. As a
matter of fact, I do not necessarily want or need a service.
I want to be cremated and I do not want a headstone of any
kind, placed any where. Scatter my dust to the winds,
wherever you deem appropriate. My heart will be in your
heart and in your memories, and that is perfectly fine
with me...
For those of you who should not be present, YOU know
who you are... You have proven time and time again, that
you do not care, so do not act as if you do now...and all

Liars and Cheaters are not welcome in my life or in my
death! Especially you, Bob.

I love you, my adorable children, granddaughters and Dad.
You are in my heart.
Thank you for everything.
Thank you, my brother, for helping me, tolerating me,
advising me. I love you, too.
You are a kind and loving person.
I love you, all my true and honest friends...

I truly have no regrets. But I have always wished that
I was just a bit taller.
Oh well, such is life.
I lived adventurously...

I meant to do the dishes.
I meant to vacuum.
I meant to paint my nails.
...To email more friends, to respond to more texts...
...To get the locks changed again...
I wanted to go to Scotland, Ireland, Australia, Paris,
England, Machu Picchu, New Zealand, Alaska and Pitcairn
Island, but I can see all those beautiful places
in my eternal dreams.
My heart will settle somewhere warm.
With a maragita, of course.

If I win the lottery today, I would buy a camper and
travel...or...if I was wealthy enough, I would fly
everywhere and take my loved ones with me.

I ate a small bowl of wheat cereal and two small cookies.
Not the best of breakfasts, but life is too short anyway.
Eat what you want and often...

I had a large sip of an energy drink, which I believe
somewhere deep down, is pure poison. But it gives me the
burst that I need to function.
Is coffee truly better?
Lately, I have been feeling quite blue and somewhat
physically depressed, for I am facing another day
alone...another week, another dreaded wintry season and
major holidays alone...again...
I ate an apple, some peanut butter, a handful of almonds
and dried cranberries. Plus, I munched on a few potato
chips, a major weakness of mine. My justification is that
since I have low blood pressure, my doctor told me to eat
things that have more salt.
How freaking awesome is that???

I downed a B-12 chewable, a mutli-vitamin chewable, a
baby aspirin, a ginger root capsule, a maca lift (which I
don't remember what that was for) and a calcium chew (I
hate the taste of that one).

A former coworker of mine (whom I wished would have
been capable of being nicer, but her heart is black and she
is quite evil. "Bitch"), had told me that I should weigh
around 300 pounds, because I eat all day long. Perhaps in
reality, I do weigh that much!
I have always had a false self-image, not a bad self-image,
as accused of me from another former coworker.
I don't own a scale, so perhaps I am much fatter than I feel,
or perhaps fatter than how I think I look.
I suppose that could be true, so I was told such,
from three former beaus.
But they were all dicks, so perhaps not!
Is weighing around 125 or 137 pounds truly being fat?
What is the purpose of being insulted?

How LOW does one have to feel about themselves, to insult another, especially a woman like me, who is kind and loving?

I do not feel at home in my own skin today.
I never meant to be a pushover.
I never meant to hurt anyone.
I freaking hate being a "people pleaser," but it's in my DNA, so there's not much I can do about that one...
I was not able to find that one man in this world, who would be strong enough to love me, as is, and who would be strong enough to do more than just love me.
...One who does not care about height or weight, and one who doesn't have "a type."
I know now that that man does not exist, who could be strong enough to actually cherish me and find lighthearted humor in my many quirks, agitations and daily oddness.

I should not have let any of them into my heart and never again, especially if something happens to me today...

HOW COULD YOU NOT?
(November 7, 2014)

As I drove through the winding hills of Kentucky and Tennessee today, I was overwhelmed with the sights that laid before me.
The sun was barely shining through the cloud-laden sky, but managed to peak through occasionally, illuminating the beautiful fall colors that adorned the numerous trees.
I caught myself holding my breath and found that I was so overjoyed that a single tear ran down my left cheek.

My children and granddaughters came to mind, as I
continued on my path, driving the designated speed, but
feeling quite rushed, quite excited...for only a few hours
later, I was bound to see them.
I sang along to the Kenny Chesney CD that I chose, and
once "Don't Blink" came on, I used all of the strength that I
had in reserve, to keep myself from bawling.
A past conversation came to mind...
I had watched the video with the same name,
years earlier, along with a long-gone ex-beau.
His reaction was interesting, for lack of a better word.
He had exclaimed that that video was depressing,
when in fact, my reaction was quite the opposite.
I told him that it was life-affirming
and definitely most beautiful.
The song continued on...as I drove past the most beautiful
sights of mountains, waterfalls, shiny lakes and rivers...
a man walking his dog along the grassy paths of a rest stop,
clusters of birds flying and seemingly dancing on the air in
rhythm, and the sun peaking through again, with its rays
bouncing off of the gray vertical rocks, tan boulders, and
many houses with wrap around porches.
I asked myself, "How can anyone not believe in the
creation of God, and God Himself,
with all this glorious beauty?
How could you not?

THE HIGH-HEELS ARE PUT AWAY
(I wrote this poem in 10 minutes at the end of the day
on June 30, 2015)

The high-heels are put away,
The Princesses are in bed,
The Queen is on the couch,
But she should be in bed instead.

The kitchen and bathrooms are clean,
The toys and bags are at the door.
The Queen wants to get up, just to do a little more.

The hum of the overhead fan may lull her to sleep,
The droning news is on, but as always, it can keep.
She will sleep soundly for just a little while,
Happy in the knowledge that her Princesses
will leave a huge smile
On her heart and on her soul, forever and for always,
So pleased that they played together,
with pinks and purples,
All of these short days.

NEVER MESS WITH THE GIRL ON THE LEFT
(Written on June 30, in the morning. I was walking by a
photo, positioned nicely among my other framed photos in
my hallway, and something hit me.
Not only does this photo make me laugh, it also makes me
wonder, "What were my parents thinking?")

NEVER mess with the girl on the left.
She showed up with a deservedly attitude.
Her physique, through no fault of her own,
hindered her desire to feel like a bride...
With wantings of white adorning her galore,
she had no choice but to show up in her hideous pink,
purple and polka dots.
This outing, right-of-passage event, celebration to some,
but not to her, was a pivitol beginning of many to come.
Her physique, through no fault of her own, would be the
subject of many teasings, many insults,
which in turn contributed to her growing snake skin.
Her desires continued for white adornment, for
compassion, for cooperative hair and a frame of thin.
But as she grew, in adventures, creativity, experiences, and
wisdom, she realized that those assets
and the compassion and more than tolerance of friends,
was what she needed to thrive.
Insults be damned, she'd cry.
My life is worth living, for I have no limits
when I reach for the sky.

RANDOM THOUGHTS:
(mid-November)

*Shocked and Rested: Sometimes it's a shock to wake
from a nap that you didn't intend to take, but at the same
time you feel rested...
*Pizza and Cake: I'd like to tell everyone that if you have
pizza and cake, I'll be right over...
*Necessary and Evil: Your job...
*Hopeful and Possible: The Lottery...
*Want, Need and Do-able: The Beach. Any Beach...

RANDOM THOUGHTS:
(early December)

*It's hard to drive when crying...
*Dad need never tell anyone that Ohio experienced
hoarfrost last night. Ever...
*I think I am going deaf in my left ear. Why one
and not both?...
*When one is poor and their family is away and/or they're
busy with other things, it's hard to get into
the spirit of Christmas...
*When one is poor, and their first family is estranged after
their mother's death, it's hard to get into
the spirit of Christmas...
*My mother has been gone for 10 years. .Why does it seem
like yesterday?...
*I find no need to put up a tree...
*Hugs and kisses are necessary to live a healthy life. This
opinion is made in reference to all and any hugs, from
anyone, including from kids to lovers...

*All of my exes were lousy kissers. .I wonder if a good-
kisser is out there for me...
*Why doesn't anyone call to check on me?...
*Oh, yeah (as my brother's comment echoes in my ears),
"They don't care!"...
*I've yet to be invited to a NYE party? I wonder
why that is...

RANDOM THOUGHTS:

*Gotta collect boxes, to pack, reduce, donate and to get
ready to run all over the world...
*I wonder what today shall bring, as I work in a difficult
and awkward situation...
*Praying today and every day...
*Who wants to go to a movie with me soon?...
*It's hard to count one's blessings, when one's hands are
tied (especially when one is used to counting
with one's fingers)...
*If home is where you hang your hat, what happens to
those of us who have no hat, no hook, nor a place to truly
call home?...
*I believe in reincarnation...and I also believe that
I was, and I am, a gypsy...

MERV
(late December, I wrote this in 30 minutes. Quite funny)

One unhappy, starving grandmother am I,
For my Tupperware is empty and my cupboards are dry.
I cook what I can, and what I have to eat,
I'm tired of peanut butter and I'd rather have
some steak meat.

I'm tired of plain 'ole bread, tired of popcorn for dinner,
I may be driven to stealing food, but I ain't no sinner.
I'm trying to stay hopeful, light-hearted and glad,
But my head is quite pounding for I feel mostly mad.

I haven't yet resorted to dog food for a meal.
I probably couldn't afford it, I'd probably have to steal.
It makes me sad that I had to think about it for a minute.
And I'm not really sure if there's actually meat in it.

When is this poor streak for me gonna stop?
It's been going on and on that my head may just pop.
I'm working two jobs, like since forever and always,
I'm never available to go to movies or even to go see plays.

What I make for all of my hard work seems
quite insulting to me,
I cannot stand working at places where I have to ask
permission to go pee.
My twelve year old managers require that I call them "sir,"
My mother's voice echoes, "I have underwear that's
older than her."

I'm never asking for laziness or for a free ride anywhere,
I'm realizing more and more that life is just not very fair.
What I want may seem trivial, may seem quite out of place,
What I want is some rest and a not-so-tired face.

I have an able body, limbs that are capable of most things,
I'd like to keep it that way, I would just like
to add some wings.
I want to travel, eat exotic foods, swim the oceans galore,
I want to tan on a white sandy beach,
near the tides and on the shore.

I like to work, I have to work, I really see no relief in sight,
Especially when I make such horrible income,
morning, noon and night.
For years I cannot make headway, I've thought of
robbing a bank.
But I'd look terrible in orange, living in a cell that's
dark and dank.

Do I just accept what has been dealt to me this fine hour,
Or do I yell to the rafters that my life
cannot remain this sour?
I am capable of creativity, of compassion,
love, and kindness.
Why has this happened and how do I get out of
this endless mess?

Besides needing better income, I'd love to find
an honest man,
Who would not lie and cheat, but love me
and be my biggest fan.
Perhaps having someone to cuddle with
and to come home to at night,
May be the one thing that I need, so I don't feel the need
to take flight.

For some time now, with all the crying,
I've wanted to give up and run away,
But the smiles of my children and grandchildren

are what makes me want to stay.
But if it's not a man for me, to love and to hold,
cherish and serve,
I think that I'll just get a huge, fluffy dog,
and I think that I will call him Merv.

He will be the one who I'd really work the hardest for,
Taking care of him....and not having him care
that I am poor.
He will be my cuddle-buddy, fed, warm, safe and dry,
He would never criticize me, so I'd have no longer
a need to cry.

Merv will love me unconditionally,
never cheat and never lie,
I will love him forever and always until the day that I die.
Merv won't mind my ongoing rantings,
babbles and endless chatter,
He will look up into my eyes, as if asking,
"What's the matter?"

I will share with him all of my deepest, darkest
secrets and dreams,
He will find ways to encourage me, not discourage me,
so it seems.
Unlike all the ex-beaus, who have cheated, a dog is where
it's at, I tell myself today,
If only I can afford him and believe that he will love me
enough to want to stay.

He won't care about my thinning hair, my cellulite and
sagging breasts,
We will sit upon our couch, watch movies,
and he will sleep upon my chest.
We will binge on Criminal Minds, Law and Order, Bones
and Friends,

With each passing day it will be our hearts
that would be on the mends.

We will turn grey together, and eat baby food when all of
our teeth fall out.
Our acceptance and love for each other will be what
Life is really all about.
This will be my last Love, not one more beau,
not even six or seven.
We will walk together across the threshold of glorious
Doggy Heaven.

LINGER LONGER
(Some of these poems and narratives are quite random,
from December to November.
I am sure that I had a lot on my mind)

I can't help but ponder,
As I've lingered longer,
More than I wanted,
More than I should.

But my mind won't let go
Of what it already knows.
As I waste my time thinking
About my lost love.

I'm sure that I do not cross his mind
Whatsoever.
The urge to cry dimishes with each passing day,
But for the realization is here to stay.

He never loved you, my mind would say,
For if he did, he would not have strayed.
He never loved you, my mind would linger
As I often give him the mental finger.

But you loved him, my mind would say
And then it wouldn't stop there.
You loved him deeply but you must move on,
For if you won't, with each passing dawn
Your heart will falter, it would feign
For your true love is on the horizon.

It is you, You are your one true love.
Be all you can, for you never needed him.
Be all you can, you must not give in
To the realization of his ultimate sin.

It is true, that he never loved you,
It is true, that he cheated and lied.
Let go of this swirling pain,
Let your heart stay untied.

No more lingering in this empty place.
Puff out your heart like the cheeks on your face.
Let your own love come rushing in,
Accept yourself, right now, as is.

You must not linger any longer,
Live your life, day to day,
And put him where he belongs,
In his own mental grave.

THE GROTESQUE, STATUESQUE, PICTURESQUE OBELISK

You get the picture.
You've seen it before.
The Obelisk is small and grotesque.

The next sighting, it's large and picturesque.
You'd like to admire it from afar.
But your curiosity got the best of you.

What can this be compared to,
When I gaze upon the mysterious Obelisk?

Nothing, except the majestic mountains
that I hike weekly,
And weakly,
And the rivers in which I have bathed and drank.

The next sighting, it's statuesque,
Which makes it quite intimidating.
Its twisted personality does not match
Its statuesque demeanor,
But my curiosity got the best of me.

If I were a giant I'd break down that Obelisk
With one chop, but my desire to do so wanes.
I'm more comfortable and satisfied with the grotesque
And this grotesque Obelisk fits perfectly within
The majestic mountains in which I must hike
And in which I must bathe and drink.

A NON-DATE, I'M SURE

When we agreed to meet for coffee I was as giddy as a
school girl could be.
The anticipation welled up inside me for over five days.
Despite feeling giddy, I felt silly as well,
for I was way over fifty,
But feeling hopeful.

Could he be The One?
Too early to tell.
Could he be kind-hearted and not be a liar
and a cheater like the others?
Too early to know.

Advice was dished, to go slow, take your time,
make him browse and want.
Going slow at Everything is quite the impossible
feat for me.
My heart is fast-paced.
My thoughts and ideas are fast-paced.
My mind is fast-paced.
My mouth is fast-paced.

My life is fast-paced.

But yet...the anticipation grew.
I looked forward to seeing him.

He came into my work on a weekly basis,
looking darn cute as ever.
How dare you?
He came into my work, giving me hope,
conversing about everyday things
And smirking that wonderful smirk
that made my heart melt.

"Grow the HELL UP," I'd scream in my head.
A man that attrractive must have someone as attractive,
In his thoughts,
In his life,
In his mind,
In his bed.
So it is, within the unwritten law of the land.
So it is, so it shall be...as it is what it is.

So as the weeks passed, I made myself try
to see him for what he was:
Just a man, with flaws and baggage, and hopes and dreams,
like everyone else.

As I went to bed each night, I dreamed of his smile,
And a smile came across my face
as I wandered into slumber.
Somewhere in my deepest dreaming thoughts,
fear crept into my soul.

I just cannot be hurt again.

Once wake would find me, I'd go about my day as usual.
The humdrum of it all...

It was a Monday, I believe, when he came into work
looking a bit haggard,
But his beautiful smile offset his temporary shaggy look.
I could see that he was nervous.
I could see that he was hesistant.
I immediately knew, from the dilation of his eyes,
That he saw me as the attractive one.

"Please don't say that you find me intriguing,"
I whispered in my head.

He asked to meet me for coffee, and I agreed.
It was obvious that he was relieved when I said "Yes."

My heart leapt.

A smile so big came over his face.
His eyes lit up and I swear that there was a bounce
In his step when he departed.

"Wow," I thought, "Just, wow."

Five days later...and it was time.
After work, we met at a nearby coffee shop.
He was already there, sitting and waiting in anticipation.

He never stood up to greet me or shake my hand,
As I believe that he should, as I feel that I am entitled to,
As a man should do, want to do, should know to do,
As his decent parents should have taught him...

His coat was on the floor at his feet, which as well,
was covered in mud.
I could smell his garlic breath from across the room.
"Make a damn effort, you, Man, you,"
I screamed in my head.

He never stood up...

My heart was pounding, my hands were sweaty,
my head began to ache.
And just like that,
He was just like the polar bears that one admires
at the zoo.
Too cute.
Too cuddly.
Too animalistic.

He was drinking coffee already, and motioned for me
to get my own...
My head snapped back and an uncontrollable "huh?"
escaped my lips.
He was munching on a cookie,
with half of the crumbs falling
On his unkempt shirt and on his half-cocked necktie.

Polar bears are nice to look at,
but I wouldn't want to be involved with one.

He was just like the puppy that you see in the window, but
once you bring them home,
You have to train them, water them, actually sit with them
and they eventually pee all
over your nice new area rug and carpet.

Stand up...and shake my hand...
Stand up...and give me some courtesy...
Stand up...and at least act like a gentleman, if possible.
What about the "pull the chair out for a lady" thing?
But No...

Puppies are cute to look at,
but I just don't have the time to raise one...

And just like that, with a snap of a finger,
I labeled this another Non-Date.
It was just another meeting for coffee and crumbs.
It was just another meeting, that I could see in those
pretty eyes of his...
That he was expecting more.

Sorry, but No...

It was just a fishing expedition,
a meeting where he was testing the waters.
That I could see in his eyes...
But I don't fish...and haven't had a desire
to ride in a dingy,
Especially without oars,
When I know that I deserve a yacht.

I was kind, I was patient,
as we chit-chatted for exactly 15 minutes,
Upon my choosing.
And just like that...it was over.

His smile still stays with me, to this day,
for after that Non-Date,
I found another job, in another state.

COACH

Coach gave me advice, the day that I met him.
We knew nothing of each, prior to that day.
I was working on a project,
He was surfing the web.

We struck up a conversation, perhaps because
We were in close proximity of each other,
Sitting and wandering with intent.
...Perhaps because of the need to fill the silence...
But mostly because we sensed a kinship with each other,
Just from one quick glance, from just a feeling
that we had had...

I asked what he was doing there, on such a cold,
late Sunday.
He told me that he needed to just get out
of his dark and dim house,
And that he needed the false sunlight
that those lightbulbs provided.
We laughed.
Somewhere in my soul I agreed,
especially the need to get out.

I told him, in kind, that I was meeting a deadline,
With finishing my transcript, to submit that same night.
Then Coach asked me if he could give me some advice.
"Absolutely," I replied.

So with brawn and bluster he loudly cited:
"You must go forth... Balls out!!
Hit the pavement running and don't look back.
Contact everyone you know,
and tell them that you love them.
Go door to door, if you have to,
network and find new clients,
New customers, new contacts and new friends.

Show whatcha know.
Tell whatcha know.
Share whatcha know...
And educate the kids with your knowledge, experience,
Education, adventure and employment.
Go for the gusto!
Never quit."

He took a deep breath, and continued,
"Never let anyone say that you Can't,
And take Can't out of your vocabulary.
I know I just met you, but I can tell that you will go far.

I see determination, not intimidation, in your eyes,
I see gratitude, not shyness, in your soul.
I see resilience and confidence in your demeanor.
I can see the future clear, I can see that you will go far."

"Wow," I thought...and offered up my hand.
He readily took it and shook it.
I promised to keep in touch with him,
as he handed me his business card.

And as I finished my project and turned to thank him again,
He was still engulfed in surfing the web,
Picking his nose and wiping it on his pants.
"Now that's a man's man," I thought.

I took his advice to heart, gathered my things,
And faded into the darkness of the hour,
Into the darkness of the night.
As I drove home, I thought,
I'm not sure about the "Balls Out" comment,
but regardless,
"Good advice, Coach. Good advice, indeed."

ADULT HOOD

I don't consider myself a lazy person,
But today I wanted to run away from
My hometown called Adult Hood.

I cry all the time, I have a lot of headaches.
I dread waking, knowing full well that I have to go to work.
My belly is bloated, for I hold my stress there and there.
I suspect that my coworkers suspect
That I might be expecting...

I feel quite trapped...again.

I'm not expecting postal reactions, but I fear
That one day soon, I am just gonna walk off the job.
I'm gonna hang up my nametag and go.
If that were to occur, I'd cry like a baby
As I walked to my car, with my head down.
Preferrably, I'd wait to cry once I got home.
But, alas, I am weak...and I am also quite poor.

I want to sell my things, pack my car with what remains
And drive south.
I hate the winter.
I want to leave Adult Hood
And live with minimal materialistic items,
Living like a beach bum,
With permanent sun-damaged skin.

I'd readily adjust to the Rum.
I would wholeheartedly give into the urge
To wear sunscreen.
I would learn to play the guitar, eat mangos,
Dance on the beach and
Fall asleep with the sound of the ocean waves

Echoing in my naive, little ears.

Would this make me happier?
Would this make me look and feel less old?
Would this envelope me in less stress, or no stress at all?
I am not so sure,
But north-be-damned, I'd be willing to give it a shot.
That is the kinda shot I'd prefer,
Compared to the shot that I have thought about,
As in a bullet to my own work-induced headaches.

People on the beach look so much more
Happier and content.
Could this be false advertising?
I want to visit their Hometown of their Adult Hood.
Perhaps they dream of my Adult Hood, as being a cure
For their headaches and woes.

Warmer is better, south is better, I tell myself daily.
The cold makes me feel old, the cold I would like to scold.
My place is in the sun, dancing free in the wind,
Dancing freely under the stars as they represent
My own special spotlight.

As I sit on my lonely couch, nightly from
My humdrum work,
My mind escapes my Adult Hood,
And is transformed into my rightful place,
Of warmth, serenity, peace and contentment,
Being surrounded by happy people, kindhearted souls,
Positive-speaking humans,
Who embrace me and welcome me,
Into their place and space, of South Adult Hood, USA.

RED FLAG, AVERAGE MAN

I was in awe that five months had already
passed so quickly.
You weren't strong, you weren't weak,
You possessed nothing more than an Average man.

However, as we had spent so much time together,
It was bound to happen.
I fell in love for the first time, as an adult.
All these years later, you still haunt me so...

You did not deserve me, my time, my heart, my love.
Average man, you still disgust me,
from your cheating and your lies.
Average man, you are below average now.
You exist, just to spite me.

Lying in your arms, those many years ago,
We talked after making love, curled up,
Wrapped up, naked in the dim room.
I thought my voice was silent, but instead I spoke my heart,
"I love you," I whispered, then realized that my words
Had echoed off of the cream-colored walls...

When I realized it, you immediately
Sensed my embarrassment,
As my body heated up, from head to toe.
We giggled, but you never verbally reciprocated,
As my face and body turned red.

That was my Red Flag, waving in the wind,
A blown-up balloon, of scarlet, crimson, brick and blood.
And my life has remained red, Average man, ever since...

Ten years have passed, with no whispers of affection,
Not coming nor going, for I deliberately remain
In the Red.

The Red Flag keeps a-flying,
The blown-up balloon keeps a-climbing,
For once either may get pricked,
With a thorny needle, a come-hither stare,
My remains in red may turn pink
And Pink is not my color.

FURNACE MAN
(Reader beware, cussing commencing)

All I said, was that I was interested in finding
someone to date, to fall in love some day,
and perhaps to eventually get married again,
as we continued our conversation about life,
family, and future.
I believed that we were engaged in "small talk."

Years later, as I called him for his furnace services again,
regarding my need for a part, for another furnace,
I met him on a snowy Saturday at his shop,
on the east side of town.
It was a light dusting of snow, as I pulled into
the back parking lot.
I had a bounce in my step...

He told me that he had some time to help me,
before he had to fix a furnace south of town.
The lights were out, the shop was quiet,

there were no bodies about.
I apologized to him, for I immediately realized
that his store wasn't opened for business on Saturday.
But, still, I thanked him for selling to me
this single twenty dollar part.
For my need of it was grand.
It was winter, after-all, and the furnace wasn't working...

And low and behold, his ignorance and sliminess
revealed its f*cking ugly head.
He told me that he had been thinking about me
since we saw each other last, that he took it as a sign
that I was really out for "a suck and a f*ck,"
on a snowy Saturday...
In the dark...
sans heat and lights and common, goddamn sense.

What-The-F*ck?

He told me that he had a couch upstairs
and was willing to service me, right then and there.
I was taken aback and his enormous physique
became all too apparent.
I could barely breathe, I took a step back,
I focused in on his face, and my concerns of my personal
safety became all too clear.

"Oh My God!" I exclaimed,
"I never gave you that impression!
Aren't you married?"

"Yes. So what?"

"Oh my god, I give you one order
from this moment forward:
Go home, kiss your wife, tell her that you love her

and ask her for forgiveness for being such the f*cking pig!"

"You should be ashamed of yourself," I continued...
(Breathe)...
"I never meant <u>that</u> and I truly believe
that you know <u>that</u>, and I don't do <u>that</u>."

I left with furnace item in tow, citing,
"Bill me," as I walked out.
I was aware that I was breathing shallow, that my skin was
as pale as the new snow that had just dusted my car.
My heartbeat was out of sinc,
as I trudged with deliberation from his shop.

"What did I say to give him that impression?
No, don't think that.
He is a pig."
I knew that the fault was his. Not mine.

Weeks later, I received the bill,
issued by a family member who worked for him.
It was 50% less than originally quoted.
I felt that much more insulted...again.

PANAMA CITY
(a very adult, short, story)

We arrived late in the day, and got cussed out for it.
This was the start of a few days in Hell, in Panama City.

After driving for more than seventeen hours,
on our 7-day adventure south, we got lost a few times,
irritating each other with our choices

of music and fast-food.

We finally checked into the No Tell Motel.
It was equipped with a mossy, filthy pool out front,
laden with undiscovered bacteria, I'm sure.
Once inside, I discovered that our room had
fuzzy wall paper, a moldy shower curtain, and truth be told,
cockroaches in hiding, waiting to come out at night
to deliberately scare the crap out of me.
There was a bent quarter stuck in the machine
that was hooked up to the bed...

Her beau was pissed at our tardiness,
but quickly recovered when she kissed him.
He went back to work for a bit, and we unpacked,
napped and showered after jacking up the air
conditioning unit, setting it on "polar."

We relaxed, watched TV and waited.
He was tardy as he came back to see us,
but we never bitched a fit like he did.
He drove, since he knew the area,
as we agreed to go out to dinner,
and it was nice, although only for a quick moment...

We went to the beach, and I got some
great shots of the ocean at sunset.
And it was nice...
Then we retired back to the motel, me alone in my large
bed, and the two of them together in theirs.
We fell asleep despite watching some mindless TV.

Around 2:00 A.M., my toes curled, my breathing stopped,
the hair on the back of my neck rose, as I heard the
unwanting advances of him on her...

My eyes rolled. Really?
I'm in the bed right next to y'all. Really?
I fell back asleep as I slowly and deliberately plugged my
ears with my fingers.

Some time must have passed, but it was still late at night,
when I awoke to him in <u>my</u> bed. He was rubbing my back
side, too low for comfort, as I had laid on my belly,
once I was asleep.

I'm like, "What the f*ck are you doing?"
But the words never came out like I had wanted.
"Stop," came out, in such a command, that my tone even
scared me.
"What are you doing?" I asked, quietly.
He proceeded to tell me that he was tired of begging, as his
advances were sturnly shot down by her.
However, his begging commenced in my ear.

Even to this day, I am not exactly sure why my reaction
was not bolder as it should have been. I have since
surmised that I was quite frozen in shock and fear.
Thinking of my friend, who was still asleep, I whispered to
this Ogre, that he must exit my bed immediately.

I was to be married in two weeks, as I reassured the Ogre
that there would be hell to pay, for I had a large family and
many friends who would be more than willing to kill him
and bury his f*cking body in the woods.

He begged again, citing that she had turned him down.
"Why did my parents not teach me some martial arts?"
I screamed in my head...
I repeated my need for him to exit my bed immediately.
I repeated my promise of killing him.

I added that I would be more than willing to find a knife in
the kitchen and stab him on the spot.
I reassured him that nobody would fault me for that...
I cited that his behavior was less than that of the gentleman
that I had thought he was...

The entire time I know that I was not breathing...
My heart was pounding so hard, that I fully expected it to
leap out of my tight chest. Moments passed,
as he begged again.
"No."
Then finally...he apologized, rolled over onto his back,
relieved himself of his urges, then patted me on the head,
as he also kissed the back of my head...

"Dear God, what just happened?"
He got out of my bed, went to the bathroom, showered,
dressed and left... It was still quite dark outside.
And the entire time, I was still frozen, lifeless...as anger,
disgust, fury and revenge welled up inside of me.

My breathing eventually returned, I jumped out of bed, ran
to the door, double-locked it and ran straight to the
bathroom where I regurgitated, cried and showered my
disgust away. I remained angry for several hours...
One might say, for even decades.

By the time that I had finished in the bathroom, my friend
was up, watching TV, eating donuts, and behaving as if
nothing was wrong. I concluded that she did not know that
her Ogre had approached me while she was in slumber.
Now came the hard part: Me telling her...

As I told her, she would not believe.
As I told her, her anger grew toward me.
As I told her, she admitted that she had nowhere to go...

As I told her, she admitted that she had lied to her mother
about our trip...about our adventures...and about her Ogre.

"How did this become the focus of what just happened?"
Pause...
"We must leave immediately. We must hit the road back
home. I want to go home!" I screamed, on deaf ears.
She insisted that we stay, she insisted that she wanted to
hear his side of the story... She insisted that she could not
return home, for several more days, due to her own lies to
her mother.

"Why did my parents teach me not to be rude?"
"Why did my parents not teach me to recognize assholes?"
We continued to argue for a bit, but soon I lost that battle,
for she reassured me that she was the owner of the car
that brought us south, that she was in a hard spot for lying
to her mother, that she was not going to assist me, as I
begged her to take me home.
And she was not going to assist me with getting to a bank,
to receive wired money from my parents who she insisted
that I not call for help...

I was quite trapped...as I was many states away from home.
And without money, without transportation, without
education, without experience on such matters.
I was not breathing...
And I felt that I could die right there on the spot.
I was duped into believing that this person was my friend...
She was no longer my friend, that f*cking bitch.
I was given no other choice... And for the next few days,
I was in complete survival mode.

The Ogre's bitch announced that we needed to get out and
sightsee, so that is what we did. We went to an amuzement
park, then we went to the beach to swim. We packed a

picnic lunch, soaked up the sun, window-shopped on the boardwalk, and I took photos, behaving like nothing was wrong, burying my need to scream and cuss and cry.

We met the Ogre for dinner, where she confronted him about the story that I had told her. Surprisingly, he freely admitted what he had done, as well as apologized and begged for us not to leave. Then came more surprises for me, then came more lies for me to hear.
"My parents sure did me a <u>disservice,</u> by teaching me to be nice," I thought, for I wanted to hurl myself over the dinner table and choke the shit out of both of them.
But, no...

His car was in the shop now, he stated, so he needed to borrow hers. His paycheck was lacking, so he needed us to move into his dorm, for he couldn't pay for the No Tell Motel, as he promised...to her. She had lied to her mother about our trip. She had told her mother that we were staying with an aunt of mine. She had told me that she had paid for our stay at the motel. For our entire trip. She told me that she had no more money.
Unfortunately, we were in that same boat.

Stress welled up inside me. Acid dumped into my stomach. I realized that I was holding my breath. I felt completely trapped, and knew I had no choice, as I stated that I'd stay on one condition: That the Ogre needed to stay his distance from me, or I'd feel free to kill him.
They agreed.

With grand hesistation, we left the strange safety of the motel room, ventured forth onto the highways and byways on the drive to the confines of his dorm room. I did not know what <u>else</u> to expect. I never had anticipated such a situation in all of my twenty-one years of existance.

It was exceptionally hot, in Panama City.

On the drive, I was eerily quiet, as I soaked up the ocean views, the quaint shops, souvenirs galore, tiny hovels and seashell-adorned homes...white sands, beach umbrellas, bouncy beach balls, seagulls, fishermen, yachts and boats rocking on the waters, as we passed by...
I wanted to jump out of that moving car.

They parked the car, we gathered our things, climbed the stairs to the third floor, walked the narrow outside balcony walkway, then entered his room.
"You've got to be kidding me," I thought.
He had a roommate: A large, football-player-sized roommate. Two twin beds...
Now what?

The Ogre stated that he'd sleep on the floor, while his friend, the bitch, and I were to try to sleep together on his twin bed. The roommate was not to be bothered, that was clear. He did smile, however, and acknowledged our existence. He would sleep in his own twin bed.

The day continued on like possibly any other day, except now it was night. Except now I was speechless. The Ogre asked for us to join him in the dorm's Rec room, down the walkway, just a few dorms away. We agreed and ventured out with him.

There I met the most wonderful of humans: Military men. There I felt safe. There we stayed for the better part of the night, eating pizza, downing pop, watching mindless TV, and being entertained by the guys and gals playing Air Hockey, Pool and Darts.

These were gentlemen, I convinced myself, sitting upon the brown leather couches and chairs, as I chit-chatted with them, about their day, their families, their friends and their jobs. I got to know quite a few of them, and was taken aback by their kindnesses, and by their "Yes, Ma'am" responses.

I never saw them as Ogres, so the ice surrounding my heart began to melt a little. My guard was still up, but not as much as just hours before. We stayed into the wee hours of the night, but then I announced that I needed to sleep. I realized that my hesitation was going back into his dorm, where anything was possible to happen.

It was clear to me that my safety was at risk, for it was clear that my well-being was not of the utmost importance to this person I once called Friend. Being before cell phones and GPS, no one knew where I was.
Hell, I didn't know where I was, specifically.

Reluctantly, we left. I readied for bed, dressing for winter in sweatpants and a long-sleeved shirt. The a/c was on high, but I was sweating with fear. I wondered at my reflection in the bathroom mirror, as I brushed my teeth, "Will I survive the night?"

The roommate slept in his bed, the Ogre slept on the floor, my supposed friend and I slept in the twin bed, with me against the wall, curled up with my own pillow, eyes wide open, praying, as I finally fell asleep, listening to the dull sounds of two males and one female snoring out of unison.

To say the least, as I awoke, I realized that I was going to need food and caffeine. Obviously, I didn't sleep well.
I had smelled coffee and bacon, as I also had heard the sizzling in the kitchenette.

I jumped up and over my still-sleeping friend, the bitch, I grabbed my clothes, rushed to the bathroom and got dressed for whatever was going to happen to me that day.

I was coming out, as she was going in... I tidied up the bed, plopped on its edge and watched the TV like a zombie. The roommate was gone, probably to work, I concluded. Like the Ogre he was, he came out of the kitchen, with a plateful of his own food, citing for me to go help myself. "Please let there be poison in my food, and end this Panama City Hell, right now."

I did just that, helping myself to scrambled eggs and orange juice only. She came straight to the kitchen and got some, too. We sat in silence, on the edge of the bed. I heard the TV...and chewing. There was lots of loud chewing. I was quite irritated.

They made an announcement that they were going to go to the mall, perhaps to lunch, that he had taken off of work, to hang out with us. Feeling trapped either way, I declined to join them, citing that I would hang out in the Rec Room all day, if necessary. I made the request, for them to give me a key to the dorm and for them to be right back after lunch. They agreed.
Were these liars to be trusted? Probably not, but I did not want to be in their presence any longer than I had to be. This decision to stay put, was a bad decision...

They got ready and left, handing me a key and a fake smile upon their exit. I dolled up my face, brushed and flossed, and ventured out onto the outside walkway and made my way to the Rec room. As early as it was, it was already bustling with music and excitement, with TV sports and Rec room activities and food.
And Military men.

I met up with some of the same gentlemen who were there
just the night before. We reintroduced ourselves, chit-
chatted and cheered on whatever sport was on the TV at the
time. We munched on snacks, we played Air Hockey,
Darts and Pool.
I was never approached in any rude manner.
I was never propositioned.
I was never talked down to...
I was never insulted.
They were gentlemen.
Then in came Rose.

Rose was a very skinny black woman, with a beautiful
smile and black shoulder-length hair. We hit it off right
away, talking about family, where we were from and about
living near the Ocean. I considered her the lucky one. She
confessed that she missed the changing of the seasons, that
we experience in the north.

Not too far in the distant future, I came to realize that Rose
was sent into my life, as my Protector. An angel. She was
kind, had a great laugh, encouraged me to go back to
school, although she knew that I was going to get married
and perhaps have kids some day soon.

Lunchtime approached, and I announced that I was going to
go back to the dorm to eat some salad that awaited me in
the fridge. Everyone said, "Hurry back." So I tried...
I looked forward to seeing all of them again.
Especially Rose.

I went to the dorm, put some salad on a plate, got a pop and
sat on the edge of the bed, eating and enjoying my
lunch...for a brief moment. I sat in silence...
Until...

The door flew open and it was the roommate. I could smell his alcoholic breath from across the room. He was angry... He locked the door behind him, headed towards the stereo, turned it up full volume, then proceeded to sprint my way. It happened so fast...

I reared back, he smacked the bottom of my plate, making the salad toss everywhere. I was in trouble and I was fearful of my lack of reaction.

He lunged at me, with his hands around my neck. He might have been six feet tall, but he was looking like more than ten feet tall and just as wide... He was yelling something about his girlfriend, and that his intention was to kill me for interferring with his pending nuptials. I could not speak, but was surprised by my strength, that he was lacking.

I was able to free myself out from under him, while kicking and trying to scream. I ran for the door, but he was quickly on my heels. I grabbed the doorknob and didn't let go. He grabbed me at my waist, pulling me in a horizontal position, positioning me in and under his arms. He had a football-hold on me, as I kicked and screamed and cussed and kicked some more.

I was able to break free, get the door open, but I was unable to make the sharp left turn out of the dorm, to make my way to the safety to the Rec room. He shoved me from behind, then into the guardrail that was there to protect one from falling into the yard below. He grabbed my right leg, as I held onto the rail for life, and he tried to toss me over the rail, to my suredly death, three stories below.

My screams were immediately noticed by the men and
women exercising in the yard below, as they stopped what
they were doing and began to point upwards.
I continued to scream...
Then all of a sudden...
The building began to shake, and I was already shaking, but
something else was happening...

I looked toward my left, from where I heard commotion.
There were many Military men running towards us, who
were previously in the Rec room. They were running to my
rescue and I prayed that they were going to save me from
falling. Some of them grabbed me, some of them tackled
the roommate. I heard, "Run to the Rec room," so that is
what I did...

I ran as fast as I could, down the long balcony and into the
Rec Room, for safety. I ran into the arms of a gentleman
and Rose, who asked me what was happening... I was
breathless, but was able to verbalize that I was attacked and
I needed help. Just as I got my last words out, the door
busted open with a loud bang!
It was the roommate!
Somehow he was able to escape from grips and the strength
of several strong men.

Rose stepped in front of me, screaming for the roommate to
stand down. With one motion of his barbaric hands, he
struck her hard, she went flying, she bounced off the wall
and fell to the floor. The sound of her hitting the wall still
sticks with me to this day.
She was lifeless...

Again, this out-of-control, alcoholic barbarian lunged at me
again, screaming nonsense about his fiance cancelling their
wedding, because of me... I didn't understand what he was

yelling about. I backed up, and he was tackled again, by several of my gentleman rescuers.

I went to the aid of Rose. She was not breathing. I was quickly wisked away, by one of the gentleman, as he cited the need to remove me to further safety. He promised to take care of Rose, as he escorted me quickly back to the dorm room.
To this day, I've never known the outcome of Rose, or what became of her...

I ran inside and grabbed up my things. Just then, the Ogre and his friend returned to the dorm room, and asked what I was doing. I ran towards them, grabbed the keys from his hands, and exclaimed to her, "I am taking your car and I am leaving. You've got two minutes to join me. If you are not in the car in two minutes, it's adios, mother-f*cker!"

I ran toward the parking lot, found the car, got inside, started it and jacked up the a/c. I was shaking uncontrollably. I waited for more than two minutes. Soon after, they came to the car. She asked me what was wrong and I responded in an Un-Catholic-like, manner, adding, "Get your ass in the car Now!"
They hugged each other, she began to cry, stating that she was going to miss him. I thought my rolling eyes were going to pop out of my pounding head.

She got inside, he closed the door, I put the car in Drive and drove like a bat out of hell... She again asked what was wrong. I told her to stop talking, that I would get around to telling her what had happened.
But I never did...

On the long, silent, awkward ride home, we never spoke, but listened to the radio. I stopped occasionally for food, and fuel and caffeine and breaks. I drove on instinct, on exhaustion, on anger and disgust. Within seventeen hours or so, we were at my home. I exited her car, with the car still running, got my bag from the back seat and walked away. She got out of the passenger side and made her way to the driver's side.

She loudly asked me, "What am I going to tell my mother?" My response, as I walked away, was less than lady-like.

Days later, she left me a voicemail message that she had no interest in being in my wedding. Go figure. I found someone else to take her place... She never attended my wedding. I ran into her many years later, whereas the burn was less burning.

I finally told her what had happened and she stated that she had no clue... She never apologized... She asked me to guess what the Ogre had given her, so I sarcastically guessed "an engagement ring?"
"No," she stated,
"Gonorrhea."
Wow, I would have never had guessed that one.

She was no longer with him. She was seeing another Ogre, I was sure. I showed her some pictures of my beautiful children. She stated that she was looking forward to meeting them some day.

Her life took a different turn, and we never stayed much in contact after that trip to Hell in Panama City.

RANDOM THOUGHTS:

*A guaranteed nap is when a football game is on...
*I may sit on the couch, but within minutes,
I will be laying down...
*I wish I could package and sell exhaustion...
*I've been struggling for over sixteen years...
*Where do y'all come up with "extra cash" to go to
concerts, plays, movies, to travel, go camping, buy new
things, go on shopping adventures, buy things for yourself
and others, go out to eat, spend time with friends...and fill
your gas tank for all these extra things in life?..
*I don't get it. I mean, the "extra cash" - I don't get it.
Where can I get it?...

THE SPINE

I may have been born with a spine, but over time my spine
has been disappearing.
I feel quite alone, but my lack of spine prevents me for
asking for help.
It is attached to my brain, after all.
I was taught to put everyone above myself, which in turns
makes me not selfish.
I want to be selfish, but my spine won't let me.
I suffer in silence, which my spine suffers all the more.
My back muscles ache, along with my neck, my belly,
and on and on.
My head pounds, but all of them are attached to my
suffering spine.
My spine keeps me going, only because I have to...
Supposedly, I am obligated, so someone told me.

My alarm also keeps me going, supposedly, I am obligated
to go to work.
I find no time to pamper my spine.

RANDOM THOUGHTS:

So, at work, it must be..."let's play all the horrible holiday
music at 4:00 A.M."
I might be going deaf, but I know "out of tune and
irritating" when I hear it...
How many variations of "Jingle Bell Rock" could there
really be? Seriously?...

REVOLVING DOOR
(Written on the last day in November, while on a 30 minute
break at work)

My mind is like a revolving door,
with perfectly oiled hinges, new fixtures,
that show up as energized cells and synapses.
I am not content with this arrangement.
in order to change that situation,
I'd have to be reborn, with new DNA.

The thoughts <u>pop</u> into my head uncontrolled.
The provocation is a sight, a sound,
a musical note, a smell.
In reference to sight, they appear at the same interval,
the same location.
I'm destined to take that route five days out

of the week...for now.
I know a different occupation will <u>not</u> stop
the pop from happening.

It's hard to drive when the tears appear uncontrollably
and often,
especially on a holiday, on a Sunday,
or any day that ends in "Y," for that matter.
In those instances, it's a sight, as well as a sound.
a musical note, to be exact...a reminder of what I
loved to listen to, way back when.

The smell can be of bacon or a wafting
of a similar cologne,
a combination of steak, potatoes and broccoli.
The "meat and potatoes" man...
I can't help but ask my brain, "Why do you do this
to me?" as if someone else would answer,
other than myself.

His love affected me so deeply.
And then, therefore, his lack of love, did as well.
But I cannot remove him, like a
clipping of my nails,
a haircut,
or a dirty sock that I've worn all day at my
twelve hours shifts.
But I cannot remove him, despite spending
time with many others, since him.

"Is this Hell?" I ask...
And answer, that it must be...
I feel trapped with thoughts that escape
and reappear, unwarranted.
Sometimes when I am feeling nostalgic,
I deliberately play the tunes that we sang to,

that we danced to...
A purposeful reminiscing...
And some days I handle that.
But...this day...I could not.

As I contemplated death at my own hands,
I asked, "Why?"
"Why would I even entertain that idea,
due to this murderous lover of my love?"
"Why?"
"Because of a <u>sorry excuse</u> for a human being
whom I loved, who never deserved me,
a wretch who cheated and lied...
who stole my heart, then didn't bother
to return it, in its entirety?"
I want it back.

Where is the rest of it and why does he seem
to control my destiny?
Why does he control my need to use it again,
so I can be free and clear, to give it all to someone else?
Why can't I find the means to release myself
from his grasp?
Why does this urge exist, that I cannot control myself?
Why does this urge exist...at all?

My lightbulbs go off very late.
Perhaps my brain was born with mold.
I wasn't born with a filter.
I do not desire to be out of control.
My parents did the best they could,
but did me a disservice by <u>making me</u> be kind...
My desire, my need to procreate, is over.
My desire, my need to give back to society, is ongoing.
My obligations to the world have been met...
But my need and desire to love someone...

and have them love me...
before I depart this earth,
is greater than I thought were possible.

On most days, I believe that loving someone is at least
One of the purposes of life,
to find someone,
to love someone,
to trust and have faith in someone...
for them to trust in me and and have faith in me,
for me to be enough for them,
to extend my limited circle, to let someone in,
and be whole, with them, within their life and
Vice-versa.

But...on this day...
I contemplated my death...at my own hands.
That...is something I could control...
Like not going through a revolving door.

UP AT 630AM AND STRESSED FOR WORK

She called out of the blue, upset and on the verge of tears,
begging me to meet her for a quick bite to eat, and with a
sarcastic suggestion of sharing of magnum of champagne.

I could never refuse her, my best friend, time permitting.
I explained that I was free, asking for a spare twenty
minutes so I could fold my laundry and put on my bra and
shoes.

Although she agreed, I could sense the urgency. She sighed, thanked me, and we hung up, knowing that we'd see each other shortly at our familiar, off-the-beaten path dive.

Appetizers and alcohol were waiting for me when I got there. I hugged her as I glided into our booth. She had been crying, so I reassured her that I was "all ears."

"Where can I go," she asked, "where I won't be picked on, or called odd names, and where treating me like a lady is an obvious way of behaving, an honest way of speaking to me?"

My answer was quick and deliberate, for making her laugh was something that I had mastered in our forty-five years of friendship.

"A cemetery," I replied.

We laughed, she paused, then she broke down.

"It's not my age that makes me weird. I've been an odd sort all of my life. It's dear friends like you who love me, not just tolerate me. It's not my memory failing, because I'm getting old. I can't seem to remember certain things from week to week..."

She sniffled as I handed her a napkin from the table.

"It's not my short stature that's irritating. Who in their right mind would get bothered by that? They knew I was short, or in this case, shorter than them, when they hired me."

I listened, as I helped myself to an artery-clogging cheese stick, dipped in marinara sauce, of course. I sipped slowly on my lime margarita.

They've been picking on me for months and I hate it, but I
do nothing. I'm not in a position to talk back or walk away.
I wasn't taught to talk back...to anyone. I can't afford to
leave, but if I stay, I'm gonna embarrass myself and go off
on them. Crying like an idiot, with snot flying everywhere,
I'm sure. Then, I'd definitely be out of a job.

It's the stress that's making me this way, that they've caused
me, from way back when it first started, pure and simple.
I'll take only half of the blame, for not stopping it the first
time it happened. I don't know what to do. I'm screwing
up at work and I'm afraid that I'll be fired. I just can't
handle the damn badgering, especially the sexual
comments. Especially the nasty ones!"

"You are still looking elsewhere?"

"Yes, most definitely."

"You'll find something. I'm sure of it."

"I hope so," she replied forcefully.

She emphasized that she should have sued "that envious
Bitch" from the previous school job years ago, for being a
liar and for making her life so miserable.

Boy, oh boy, I remembered that one.

She emphasized that she should have "smacked the crap"
out of that other "jealous Bitch" at the clothing shop where
she had also worked.

That, too, seemed like an undying tale.

She emphasized that she should have "buckled the knees" of the "punk co-worker" who kept making fun of her for being short.

Many late night conversations took place regarding that crap.

She emphasized that all of these transactions, and many more, were unprovoked, unwarranted, and definitely unnecessary.

I agreed.

This venting seemed to be helping her, but I wasn't seeing or hearing what I wanted.

I wasn't witnessing her backbone growing. I wasn't hearing plans for changes that she needed.

She needed to learn to stand up for herself, and to go back to school, and she needed to do this quickly...for time was running out.

(to be continued...)

RANDOM THOUGHTS:

So...how does one "get into" the Christmas spirit?
Especially...since I'm bogged down with (what seems like)
*Endless Sadness,
*Carb-inducing Crying,
*I-feel-fat-and-I-know-I'm-fat False Thinking,

*I'm-poor-and-I-see-no-way-out, smack-in-my-face-that's-just-the-way-it-is Thinking,
*Endless-chocolate Craving,
*I-truly-hate-winter Reality,
*Missing-my-family Boo-hooing,
*I-hate-my-job Mentality,
*Menopause-sucks Reality,
*I-can't-get-enough-sleep Depression,
*Can-someone-please-put-me-in-a-coma Pondering,
*I-have-no-idea-how-to-trust-my-feelings Blahs...and...
*I've-got-no-one-to-talk-to Blues?
***If I see a jewelry commercial one more time, I'm gonna throw myself down a flight of stairs.

DOWNING THE POISON

It's like a snowball rolling down hill,
A ying and a yang, a give and take,
An arm with a leg,
A neck with a necklace,
It's caffeine, and the need for more caffeine.

I didn't get enough sleep, for whatever reason,
Be it stress especially when it's work-related,
A need to watch a favorite show at late hours,
A forgetting of paying a bill,
A need for a much longer hot bath...
For whatever the reason,
I have to down the poison, that keeps me awake.

Awake may be what I literally am,
but here is where I am not.
I am a zombie with it, I am a zombie without it.

It's perpetual. It feeds itself.
It's a fire that stays in an ember state.
It is necessary. It is not necessary.

I introduced coffee into my system, within weeks of
starting a new job.
This job is stressful, was my justification.
This job is my need, was my reasoning.
I must stay awake to perform correctly.
I must be alert. I must survive.
I hated the taste. I found no true enjoyment,
For either the job or the coffee.

I graduated from coffee to energy drinks.
Then it was a pain killer with caffeine.
Then it was a concentrated caffeine burst.
But then came yummy high-calorie foo-foo drinks.
Those lasted a short while.
My belly was screaming...

To this day, I am still downing the poison,
But in smaller intervals, smaller amounts.
I finally convinced myself that my friends, coworkers,
managers and whomever,
Will just have to get less activity from me...
I am here. I showed up. I am alive.
I am awake. I am on time.
You are welcome.
I am downing the poison.

RANDOM THOUGHTS:
(mid-January)

*I seriously don't know what day it is, nor the date, and I'm
tired of not opening my curtains, because I come home
from work in the dark...
*By the way, I'm a zombie...
*My couch has become my enemy...
*I'm tired...ironically and literally...of downing
too much caffeine...
*Too bad I didn't win the lottery. It would have been epic
for me (yes, I would have been a bit selfish and I would
have bought an RV)...
*I'm thankful for my children...
*I'm thankful to be working...
*I'm thankful for my overall health...
*I need chocolate...
*I'm working on an awesome screenplay, does anyone
know Quentin Tarantino's phone number?...

GAVE UP, GIVE UP, GAVE IN, GIVE IN

I asked, "How many sit-ups do I have to do
to look like that?"
He said, "None. You'll never look like that."
I give up...

He said he loved me, which was something
that I needed to believe.
I finally said that I loved him, trusted him,
will always be there for him.
I gave in...

He found another and disappeared shortly after.
I was devastated, I didn't see it coming,
I was heart-broken.
So, I gave up...

I found peace in helping and being in service.
I found contentment in volunteering.
So, I give in...

I improved my health, I took a chance on another.
We said three words, we made a commitment.
Again, I gave in...

It was like I was with the same person,
that they're all the same.
I realized that I was back to square one.
Again, I give up...

Falling to my knees, I raised my hands to the heavens,
I cried and asked for help,
I heard, "Believe in Me. Trust in Me."
So...I gave in...and gave up...

FAIRYTALE
(This on-the-spot, made-up fairytale was told to my
children, a little at a time, over time, at bedtime, with
assorted details and scenarios...
all with quite happy endings.
For you Craig and Claire,
my inspiration and my personal cheerleaders.
Thank you)

As long as Maggie could remember, she had been coming
to this small New England town to visit every fall. Even in
her short, twelve years, Maggie never understood why her
family visited in the fall. All of her friends would have
summer vacations. She questioned her parents about this,
with every visit. No matter what, the answer was always,
"You will learn why." This was enough to drive Maggie
crazy. This was her mother's childhood town, not hers.
This dark, grey, blustery day was no different than any
other, except Maggie left the cabin, in a huff, because she
didn't want to hear that answer again.

This day, Maggie ventured out a little farther than the
previous year. She was a little apprehensive, but decided it
would have been worth it. Even the cold wind on her face
was better than just sitting in the dank boring cabin. She
walked along the beach, watching the gulls in the distance
swoop up and down along the docks. She continued to
walk, feeling the hard-packed sand under her feet. She
thought about what the beach might look like in the
summer...how the beach would be covered with travelers,
and their blankets and radios. She smiled to herself as she
continued on... Maggie was unaware of the time. She
watched as the sun danced behind he overcast clouds. She
squinted at the intense brightness.

As she continued on, the beach began to look a little more narrow than near the cabin. The ocean's surf began to get more and more powerful and a little menacing. The small cabins and businesses were farther behind her now, and she became aware of the silence. All she could hear was the surf. She began to get a little worried. "Just how far did I go?" she wondered. She also noticed that she could no longer hear the gulls.

Reluctantly, she stopped walking, took a deep breath, and turned to go home. Fear swept through Maggie as she noticed something very odd. The sun had gone down a lot faster than she had realized. She had no clear path to get home. She felt very afraid. "What am I going to do?" she thought. She stood motionless for a moment and thought about what her mother had told her about getting lost. "Stay put, or follow your footsteps back. You must make the right decision. The choice is up to you," she would say. Right then, she wanted her mother more than ever. Maggie thought that at any moment her mother and father would show up. She stood and stood and waited and waited. She began to get a chill. With the sun down, it was going to get even colder. Her bright, curly red hair was now caught up in the high winds. She couldn't control it. It was in her face and blowing everywhere. She pulled her sweater tight around her. She began to cry.

The surf on the jagged rocks was a lot louder. She began to resent her choice of leaving the cabin. Just as she was about to take a step forward to go in the direction of what she assumed was home, she heard cries echoing off of the rocks. It was faint. She forced herself to stop crying, but the echoing continued. She realized that the cries were not hers. It sounded like the cry of a small child. She strained to listen. She heard it coming from over near the rocks. She hesistated...she listened...she began to walk nearer to

the rocks to find out what was making the noise. The
closer she got to the rocks, the quieter the surf became. She
was now upon the rock face, and the surf completely
quieted. It stilled, on its own. A cloud of fog surrounded
her. She panicked and turned to run, then she heard a small
voice. "Don't leave," it said. She turned around, and there
sitting on a small stone was a dainty fairy.

The fairy was powder blue and pink. Her hair was blue and
pink, her body was blue and pink...her wings were blue and
pink. Maggie was taken aback. "How odd," she thought.
The fairy smiled at her, and said, "Don't leave. Don't be
afraid. We'll take care of you." Maggie smiled back at the
fairy. "I'm cold," she said, "And I'm lost." "I know," said
the fairy, reaching out to Maggie. Maggie offered her hand
back, and with one touch of the fairy's hand, Maggie was
reduced to the same size as the fairy. "This is our home.
We live inside the rocks. We will take care of you."
Maggie looked all around. There were dozens of fairies all
around her. They were all different shades of blues and
pinks.

Maggie was fascinated at how beautiful they all were.
They went inside. Their home was inside a cave on the
rockface. It looked like a small dollhouse with candles lit
everywhere. Their wings and dresses shimmered in the
candle light. Maggie noticed she was instantly warmed.
She asked the fairies about why they lived in the cave, and
they began to tell her about themselves, one sentence at a
time, one fairy at a time, finishing each other's sentences.
They told her about how they had always lived there, since
the beginning. They had been protected by the surf, and
they protect anyone who comes near the rocks. That is all
that they do, they told her. They have protected many
children, travelers, and beachcombers. They swore Maggie

to secrecy and for the remainder of the night, they told
Maggie about rescues and adventures, living in the rocks.

They sat near the fire in the fireplace, told stories and
provided a nice dinner for Maggie, which consisted of hot
tea, raw vegetables, fruit and pineaple upside-down cake.
Although it was getting late, Maggie was no longer
worried. She felt warm, protected and loved. Even though
she knew the surf was right outside, it was very quiet in
their cave. Maggie began to tire, so the fairies let her sleep
right there, on the hearth of the fireplace. They told her
when she awoke, they would direct her towards her home.

When Maggie awoke, the fairies were right there with her.
They told her it was time to go, and they gave her a small
ring of pastel pink roses. One of the fairies motioned to the
door of the cave and Maggie walked through it. They were
now outside, on the ocean's rocks. Although Maggie could
see the surf pounding against the rocks, it was quiet and she
was not afraid. One fairy touched her hand, and in an
instant, Maggie was back to her normal size. She was
standing in the sand, facing the direction of the cabin. She
turned around, waved goodbye to the fairies, who were all
aflutter around the cave's entrance. As she walked in the
direction of the cabin, fog surrounded her. She smiled, had
a little faith, and continued to walk. She eventually saw
what she assumed were her footsteps from the night before.
The surf's sound sang in her ears. The fog lifted and she
walked the length of the beach. She saw the cabin in the
distance and continued towards it. She looked toward the
sky and let the lowered, overcast sun beam on her face.
The wind was cold, but she did not mind.

As she approached the porch of the cabin, she saw that her
parents were sitting on the glider, rocking and sipping tea,
just like the previous day. They both smiled at her, and her

dad asked, "Changed your mind?" "What do you mean?"
Maggie asked. "You weren't gone for long," her dad stated.
"What do you mean?" Maggie asked, again. "I was lost.
You didn't come look for me. I spent the night on the
beach," chimed Maggie. Her parents laughed. "Maggie,
you were gone for just about ten minutes," her mother said.
"No I wasn't," Maggie steamed, "I spent the night on the
beach...I was taken care of by a bunch of..." Maggie
stopped herself. Her mother asked, "You were taken care
of by a bunch of what?" "Never mind," barked Maggie,
"Just never mind."

Maggie rushed into the house and ran up to her room. Her
mother followed immediately behind her, sitting on the
edge of Maggie's bed. "Maggie, what's going on? Honey,
you were gone only ten minutes. Get ready for bed. We
have a big day tomorrow," she told her.

Maggie's dad entered her bedroom. "Honey, don't make up
stories. Have a good night's sleep. I'll see you in the
morning." Maggie spoke firmly, "I didn't make anything
up, dad. I did sleep on the beach...well, actually in a cave
with a bunch of blue and pink fairies. I was lost, and they
took care of me. They gave me dinner and we sat around a
fireplace telling stories." Her dad laughed, "Oh, yeah,
right. It sounds like a story that your mom may have told
you. Go to sleep." And he walked out...

Maggie began to cry, "It's true!" she yelled, after her dad.
She looked at her mother. "It's true, mom. It's true. They
took care of me. They gave me this!" Maggie pulled the
ring of flowers from her sweater pocket. Her mother
picked them up and said, "How lovely." At that moment,
Maggie's dad peaked his head back into the bedroom
doorway, and said, "Fairies...in a cave...of course you were

telling stories... Go to bed." "Mom, I'm telling the truth,"
Maggie whispered. "I know," her mother said.

Maggie's mom pulled a thin-chained necklace out from
under the neck of her sweater. On the chain was a small,
clear brooch. Encased within the brooch was a small ring
of pastel roses. Maggie was astonished. When she looked
up at her mother, her mother winked. Her dad yelled from
down the hall, "Go to bed...we have a big day tomorrow."
Maggie and her mother laughed. "Now you know why I
like to come here," her mother began, "I was about your
age when I, too, got lost wandering away from this cabin.
I, too, was rescued by the fairies. From time to time, I
would still go visit them, and it was as if time had never
passed. Especially for them. They told me of their many
adventures and of their rescues, of children and sailors past
and currently. They kept me safe. And, of course, no one
believed me. It must remain our little secret, okay?"
"Okay," Maggie agreed.

Maggie's mother tucked her into bed and kissed her on the
forehead. She winked at her again, they said their
"goodnights," her mother turned off the light and left the
room. For the first time, Maggie felt that it was okay to
visit this small New England town in the fall. She felt a
real kinship with her mother, now that they had a secret to
share, something that she knew they had in common. She
could hear the wind whipping up outisde, and she could
hear the surf rolling back and forth on the shore. She
closed her eyes and concentrated on the muffled sounds.
She smiled. As she lay in her bed, she felt warm, protected
and loved. She knew from that moment forward, all was
going to be okay. She drifted off to sleep, dreaming of the
wonderful night that she had spent with the dainty blue and
pink fairies.

RANDOM THOUGHTS/RANDOM QUESTION:

*I just got paid, it's Friday night...
*I'm tired of crying...after all that hard work...
*Something doesn't seem fair about that...
*Car maintainence and miscellaneous bills come before
grocery shopping...
*I've lost 6 more pounds, without exercising...
*No time to eat, no time to exercise...
*Some days, breaks are not allowed...
*Something doesn't seem right, or legal, about that...
*I like to eat...
*I like to nap...
*I like to write...
*I need to move in with someone and be their roommate,
pay R&B...preferrably somewhere very south...
*I'm selling all my things...
*No time to socialize, no time to mingle...
*So sad that I haven't had time in months to go to church
because of work...
*Will my soul drift toward Hades because I haven't
been to church?...
*I like to work, I need to work...

NO FILTER

Did I just say that outloud, again?
Oh my goodness, could it be possible that I was conceived
And born, without height, but also with no filter?

I have curly hair, but I can straighten it,
Either with a device or by sticking my scissors in an outlet.
This No Filter makes me seek an outlet.

I lack inches, but I can wear high-heels,
Not too high, because I am afraid of heights.
This <u>No Filter</u> makes me want to climb the Eiffel Tower.
I inherited my chubby, pudgy midsection,
I blame my Irish ancestors...
For all of the potatoes they consumed,
has been handed down into my DNA...
A disection of this <u>No Filter</u> could be in order...

But where does this <u>No Filter</u> originate?
Too many preservatives in the American diet?
Do I have a brain tumor?
If I did, would I want to remove it?
Because on most days, I like the fact that
I speak my mind.

At work, I seem to be able to hold my tongue,
At least for one hour out of the eight.
I've not been fired.
I've not been slapped.
I have been made fun of...with a clear desire
to trip that person,
The next time I saw them...

Did I just say that outloud?
There it goes again!

The thought creeps into my brain, perhaps coming from
As far down as my shoes, if I am wearing any...
And makes its way to the edge of my tongue
and out it goes.
I can not only see, but I can hear the eye-rolling.
I can not only see, but I can hear the clothes rustling
On the body standing in front of me,
From their uncomfortableness and their awkwardness,
Out of the unacceptibleness of what I just said.

Some have accepted me for what, and for who, I am.
One would have to be a strong and unique individual,
To not only accept us <u>Non-Filters,</u> but perhaps they
Too have <u>No Filter.</u>
Perhaps I have not, or perhaps that I have, noticed,
But they are okay with not getting a word in edgewise.
Most of the time, they are not listening, anyway.
I can hear your eyes rolling, right now...

THE LOOK

Perhaps since the age of teen, there has been The Look,
from boys to men, from the young to the aged...
However, it probably presented itself within
the fog of innocence,
as I played with my dolls, played hide-and-seek,
played Tag, colored in coloring books and thought of
nothing else.

However, The Look I first took notice, was at the age
of over forty and then some, from a man
who's face never altered,
but somehow his eyes captured the stardust in my own.
There is this Look, that I have recognized, that I can now
acknowledge, from the man or men sitting or standing
at the opposite of me...

It is a Look of appreciation, of admiration; a like, if you
will, but alas, beware, it is not the same as The Look
of unholy thoughts, for that Look is accompanied
by a smirk of slight, just a smidge dip at the
corner of his mouth.

For I have seen both, and The Look is such accepted,
with acceptance, flirtatiousness, of dubious innocence
for it is in that moment that one thinks they are not worthy.
Once The Look accompanies the smirk, the cards
are thrown down on the table, the stardust is wisped away
on the winds of the twilight, but not forgotten.

That Look with its smidgen dip, is one that sends ripples
down one's spine, causes one to start to sweat, and causes
one to want to run and hide, and perhaps
even slap the sender.
That Look is unjust, unwarranted, unacceptable,
and unprovoked.
However, The Look, one that is received as a silent
Thank You, a Thank You that states that you ARE pretty,
you ARE beautiful...can be accepted for all eternity, for
when the moment rears its head, when you realize that you
are worthy of admiration and appreciation.

There is this Look, that I get, from men of young and old,
a Look of desire, and a silent Thank You, for being you.
I have received this Look, however, be aware,
that I do not give out that Look, for I am never in a position
to test the waters, of where you swim, and of where your
significant other would like to drown you...

COMPASSION ACTION

What could be simpler, than a Thank You, a door held
open, a nod of the head, that screams compassion?
It's the action of compassion, that not only makes the
receiver feel human, but benefits the giver as well.

Why weren't you taught of compassion? As I understand
that on the surface you seemed quite acceptable.
Aha, an overheard conversation with your relative and
Viola!, I understand why you have no compassion.

You are self-absorbed. You cannot hold a door open for
me, and you curse an entire race in front of me.
You are a contradiction, so you have no compassion.

Any action of compassion comes from within.
I have a "within." You are empty of a within.
Money, money, money...is all I hear from you.

Sadness, for you weren't as tall as your brother.
Oh brother, why bother being sad about that?
Helping others, is what life should be all about.
Giving to those who are less-fortunate,
should be all's order of business.

You hate yourself, but why? You are able-bodied, you
hold a bit of smartness in that pea-brain of yours.
You should exercise compassion within.
Oh, but wait...
How can I help you find your within?
Should that be my ongoing, albeit helpless, compassion
action?

LIBRARIAN

I am sure that if you weren't married, we'd be dating.
But because you are married, we won't be married.
I find sometimes that I wished I was married,
but I will not be married, because I look like a librarian.
That is what he told me.

I cannot be a librarian.
One: Because I cannot be quiet.
I met your wife, she is quiet.
I consider you very unlucky.
For a quiet woman, is a plotting woman.

It's better for me to say what's on my mind,
despite the fact that I have no filter.
I say what I want and when, so there'd be no
misunderstanding. I say what I want and when, but also,
I am no fool.

I cannot be a librarian.
Two: Because the dusty books would make me sneeze.
I met your wife, she probably doesn't sneeze. She has
enough money to pay someone else to sneeze for her. I do
know that is why you married her, Because of her money.
You married her to spite me.
I consider you very unlucky.

I cannot be a librarian.
Three: I don't look good in head-to-toe clothing.
This is the picture that I have in my head, of a librarian.
I know what you were trying to say, I know your comment
was to insult me. I met your wife, she probably told you
what to say. I will come up with the best retort, as soon as
I read all of those books, because I can be a writer
and now, a librarian.

DEATH WAS INSTANTANEOUS

I was so excited to go on this recommended date, a first for me, of no contact in advance, a new thing, nervous of my reaction and vice-versa. With red dress, black shoes, a glamorous hairdo and a new svelt body, I was owning it, as I walked into the dim-lit restaurant, ironically called Lucky's.

I asked the host to allow me to sit near the bar, but not at the bar, because I thought that would send a strange message to others, sitting there for something that I myself was not seeking. So, this cute young gentleman pulled out my chair for me, told me that Miguel would be my waiter, and asked if I needed anything, and with my negative response, he told me to have a nice meal, then scurried off.

With each moment of a male coming toward me, I wondered if that was him, my date, the one who could restore my faith in "man, oh, man, humanity."
Ooo, he looks nice. No.
He brushed passed me on my left...
Aww, he has great hair. No.
His swagger was more like mine...
Mmm, could it be?... No.
He had on a wedding ring, and, yes I looked...
Ooo-la-la... No, he was too cute, if that were possible.
The moments ticked on by...

Then, he approached my table, called my name, I stood up, we shook hands, then we sat. We smiled, the waiter came rushing over, my date ordered wine... He grabbed the skinny breadsticks and chewed with his mouth open. I could overlook that, I told myself. His green eyes twinkled in the candle-light. He snorted, then blew his nose into the burgundy cloth napkin. Perhaps he has a cold, I told myself. He laid the soiled napkin on the table, never excusing his behavior. I could overlook that, I told myself.

He was handsome enough, thank goodness. But I must admit, that he was physically too big, too intimidating for me. But...I wasn't going to let my insecurities from past lovers, past dates, past experiences, deter me from possibly a good time. He had all of his teeth, he was employed, he was over five feet tall, So I let the date commence...

I didn't think that I was shallow, but perhaps I was, perhaps I am. Or perhaps I was just fearful, as my mind wandered and wondered about the Law of Physics. Only a few moments went by, among the whole scheme of things. I could hear the tick-tock of time, I could hear myself getting closer to the end... I never considered it a waste, to meet someone, to get to know someone.

So the date continued, with small talk, and mind you, it wasn't more than twenty minutes... And with this comment, death, of the date, was instantaneous:

"I am tired of dating tall women, who are absolutely very pretty. I'm glad you are short, 'cuz I want to start dating shorter gals, like you, who aren't so caught up in their looks."

Seriously?
With my fingers, I combed my untangled, curly red hair across my forehead and nestled it behind my right ear. Simultaneously, I plopped my elbow on the table, held my head up with my forefinger and thumb tucked in between my eyes...and I just started laughing...
"Oh my god, I cannot believe that you just said that," I murmured.

"What?"

I sat back in my chair, a comfy chair at that, put my clean
napkin on my plate, scooted my chair back...bent down
toward my left foot and grabbed my purse. Placing this
tiny little matching-my-outfit purse in my lap, with eyes
wide open, I stated that the date was over, and as I stood,
his overbearing size became all too clear.

"You're not leaving. Nobody leaves a date with me."
I felt no need to state why I was leaving, so when I turned,
his sweaty large hand grabbed my left wrist.
"Oh no, you didn't," I said in my head, as I looked down at
his hand, then looked him square in the face.

"Let go of my arm," I calmly stated.
"Sit the hell down," he stated, not calmly.
"Let go of my arm," I calmly restated.
"Sit the hell down," he stated, much loudly.

As the waiter started to come over, this date yelled for him
to back off. I looked at the waiter, then all around the
room. "Everyone is staring," the gutteral sound came out
from this throat.
"Nobody leaves when on a date with me," he stated.

Suddenly, a gentleman stood up, walked over to us and told
this date to let go of my arm. His response was very
unbecoming. I must have had a furrowed brow, as I told
the gentleman that it would be okay. He never left my side,
as he repeated to this date, to let go.

At that moment, I had a couple of choices:
Sit, or don't sit.

I reassured the gentleman that all would be well, so, I faked a sit-down, and in doing so, the date let go of my arm. I took a deep breath, turned and placed my purse on the comfy chair behind me, then proceeded to let the death of the date be instantaneous.

In somewhat ninja-like fashion, I hurriedly clutched the date's necktie with my left hand, and grabbed the back of his head with my right. I slammed his face into his plate full of breadstick crumbs. I yelled in his left ear, "The date is over," as he struggled to be free of my one hundred-fourteen pound grasp. I let go and backed off, and he sat upright, but his pretty green eyes turned dark-not-so-pretty.

He proceeded to stand, as I rushed over to kick his legs out from underneath him, forcing him to resit... I backed off, grabbed my cute little purse, shook myself straight, and fixed the bottom half of my new dress. Adjusting it at my hips, I looked at him with a scold in my eyes, as if to say, "I freaking dare ya." I turned on my heels, kissed my gentleman on his cheek and sashayed toward the exit.

I apologized to the waiter, on my way out. I apologized to the host, on my way out. I walked with confindence to my car, but I am no fool. I took my time to breathe in the dampness of the night air. I looked upwards to the heavens to try to see some summer stars that may have been hidden between the historic structures that lined the brick-laden street. I was aware that my teeth were grinding, for I was baffled, again, about the instantaneous death of another date.

Why do I think that I deserve better?
Do I require a pure gentleman?
Do I need a man...to cherish me, to love me, all the remaining days of my life?

The Saturday night was a-buzz with comings and goings.
I heard music in the surrounding bars, along with chatter
and laughter. I was in a crowd, but I felt completely all
alone. Again. I wanted to rush into one of the bars and
jump right into the Karaoke. I wanted to rush into one of
the taverns, sit at the bar, order a beer and enjoy the live
bands that were featured throughout.
I wanted to call my girlfriends, to cry, to vent, to cuss,
but they were all busy with their husbands and beaus, their
families of dogs and cats and plants and...
But, alas, I felt compelled to sulk at home, something of
which I had become an expert. My mind was behaving like
a indecisive ping-pong ball on a mile-long and mile-wide
ping-pong table.

Just as I was about to cross the street, at the intersection of
Maybe and Just-Because, a gentle hand tapped me on my
left shoulder. Somehow I knew that I did not have to
become my crazy-ass, Ninja-Grandma self, so I slowly
turned, and it was my gentleman rescuer.

"Please come back to Lucky's and join us for dinner."
Without much forethought, I asked why...
"Everyone is talking about your reaction to that guy. We
were impressed by the way you handled yourself. We'd
love for you to join us. My date cancelled on me, and I'd
love to treat you to dinner."
In my head was the weird reply of, "So why the f*ck not?"
I was jumping around in my mind, like a foolish school
girl... But like the lady that I pretend to be, I replied,
"It would be my honor. Thank you."

The death, for me that night, was instantaneously over. It
was no more sulking for me on that Saturday night. I had
dinner with my gentleman and his six friends.

We talked briefly about my date and laughed,
We talked about our jobs, our hobbies and the like...
My gentleman chewed with his mouth closed.
My gentleman held the door for me.
My gentleman placed his napkin on his lap.
My gentleman leaned in and whispered in my ear,
That my faith in "man, oh, man, humanity" had been
restored...

LIFE IS PASSING ME BY: AIRPORT LIFE

As I stand encapsulated by the cash register counter,
in my required non-flattering dull attire, I see many faces
come and go. Mostly everyone is of a happy nature,
rarely an admission of death, of funeral, of surgery,
of the saying of Goodbyes.
I greet, because that is my job,
I offer, because that is my job,
I stand for eight hours, not being permitted to sit,
because that is my job. I hold my bladder and bowels, not
being permitted to "go," I tell you,
because that is my job.

Shame on the CEOs and owners of this god-forsaken set
up. I am sure that their intestines are in tip-top shape, that
they themselves are sitting each day in temperature-
controlled environments, and they don't experience the
damned deodorant failure of my daily life.

I see the crooked and straight teeth, if they have teeth,
I smell the coffee breath, and the just woke up breath of
death, As they take a deep sigh, or not, disgusted that the
prices at the airport are a damn rip-off, a crime, an "I got

you by the balls" price hike, that for some reason makes someone else richer, but not I...

I meet well-put-together gentlemen, in suits and military attire, "Thank you for your service," quickly taking a subconsious knee-jerk look at their ring finger, imagining their life and their destinations, feeling lucky to have seen such a beautiful creature, if only Oh-So briefly...
My admiration is never hidden, as our eyes meet, they are aware that I am aware that I find them quite the well-put-together catch.

And yes, I am sometimes taken aback, as I see not-so-attractive men as well. Nice, they are, but not always appealing. Beauty is in the eye of the beholder, and I am sure they are also taken aback by me, with my dark circles and my beautiful smile, regardless of lack of sleep from the many nights before.

Without fail, I have come to realize that I am putting myself in comparison to some of the females that cross my path, for I have seen beauty there as well, and for I have seen some as if in a life-in-progress, too...
I wonder sometimes if some of these patrons own a mirror... I wonder why some of these females have not gotten the memo about leggings and how not to wear them... I wonder why some have not taken the time to brush their bed head.

And I wonder if I can jet off with some of them, for I know that I can fit in the overhead bin.

I encounter many diverse individuals, asking of their journeys, or not, depending on their demeanor, their "I just woke up, so don't be cheery" attitude, depending on the time of day, depending on the nature of the smile.

I see families going to amuzement parks, singles going on
Spring breaks, patrons going to Cozumel, Honduras,
Alaska, China, and not so far out places alike.
...patrons who are excited again, and for the first time, of
flying, cruises, seeing long-lost loved ones, seeing their
newly-born family members for the first time.

I share, when appropriate, about my limited adventures, my
family, my grandchildren, as they willingly talk about
theirs, or not, with eyes beaming, or not, with excitement in
their voices and vocabulary, or not. I sit there,
metaphorically, listening with intent, of their adventures,
their varied jobs, their reasons for travel, for pleasure, for
work, for fun in the sand and sun.

Some just want the various newspaper options, and nothing
else. I don't chit-chat with those individuals on purpose.
They are always in such a hurry.

When down-time occurs, I stock, I straighten, I fold, I dust,
I cringe at the droning repetitive sounds of the god-
forsaken required DVD about the Wright Brother's claim to
flying fame. I have it memorized.
I want to kill myself as I hear it one more time.
This is borderline torture, I tell myself, to listen to this
story, over and over, again and again, day in, day out. I am
convinced that this is along the lines of a violation of my
rights for peace and contentment. Don't get me wrong, I
love the accomplishments of the Wrights, but damn!

I am positive that if given the option to trade places with
me, the CEOs and owners would not last the day for within
the inside of repetition number three, they would be pulling
out what was left of their thinning hair. They wouldn't
stand a chance. They wouldn't stand for it...
But, alas, they are where they are...

And I, am where I am...
...dealing with my life, as I watch it pass by,
at the airport...

Sometimes, it is a slow death...

As I stand encapsulated by the cash register counter, I am
surrounded by temptations of sweet things, chocolates and
gummies galore, unhealthy selections of chips, cheesy
things, crackers, mushy-mushy concoctions of super-high
caloric nightmares. I am surrounded by various periodicals
donning thin and beautiful starving and half-naked models
and celebrities, with boob shirts, swimsuits smaller than a
quarter of a table napkin...proclaiming their successes and
failures of movies, diets, relationships, and fashions.
I keep my eyes averted, for when I see the shapes and sizes,
I want to go home, cry myself to sleep and talk myself
out of suicide.

Is it no wonder that I hate my job, for it is what I do,
because it is my job, for now.
I'm freezing, I'm sweating, I have a headache on the drive
there... My belly is in a continuous knot, not knowing how
and when to relax. I pack my lunch for my wage is quite
the embarrassment. I pack my lunch for my health is at
risk. I pack my lunch, for that is what I need to do...

As I stand encapsulated by the cash register counter, I am
saddened that I have no windows... I am reminded that I
cannot see the sun, but I know that it is there. I cannot see
the airplanes take off and land, but I know that they are
there. I cannot see the puffy clouds, the thin-lipped clouds,
the storm-encased dark clouds, but I know that they are
there. I cannot see, nor hear, the rain, a light Spring
welcoming rain...
But I know that it is there...

Each night, as my head rests on my tear-soaked pillow, I
pray for a sign, a message, a reason to get up out of bed
with furvor, with purpose, to jump out of bed, like toasted
bread quickly jumping from the toaster.
When I dread the day, it is clear that I must make another
change... My mental, physical, and spiritual well-being is
at risk, as I watch my life passing me by,
at the airport.

RANDOM THOUGHTS/RANDOM
QUESTIONS/RANDOM RANTS,
on this dreary October Sunday morning:

*A week later and my back still hurts. Sciatica? Perhaps.
Or is it hurting from all of the back stab wounds that I have
received throughout my life?...
*Can one get 2nd degree burns from a heating pad?...
*Yes, I am out of shape, but it's the shape that I am in. And,
this is the God-given shape in which I was born...
*Genetics suck. I am not geneticly blessed, or so I've been
told, or so I've been lead to believe. I am tired of
fighting genetics...
*I have two words for anyone who criticizes my physique
again. And yes, I am tired of that, too...
*My visits with Dad will lighten my spirit...
*My visits in Columbus always lightens my spirits...
*My tears are Not diamonds, or I'd be a wealthy
woman by now...
*Winter is coming. I hate winter...
*My toes are cold...
*Unpacking winter garb is depressing...

*Right now, I can identify with "Someone Like You" and "Something's Gotta Give"...
*Horror movies scare me, however Halloween is my favorite holiday...
*Is there a large family out there who'd be willing to adopt me? Preferrably, one in another country perhaps? Or south? Or New Zealand?...
*I make a mean taco dip...
*I love to ride my bike...

DEAR MOM (#1)

Dear Mom,

I hope that I haven't disappointed you much. I know that you know that I have enough disappointment for a lifetime. You have seen me succeed and you have seen me fail. Today. Right now.
I would love to have your advice right now.

I feel that if you were here today, I would not have made the many relationship mistakes that I have made, that you would have somehow made me see the light and the error of my many ways...
You would have known, and scolded, the liars and cheaters, and perhaps would have threatened their lives...enough so, that they would have run away crying like school girls.

If I could talk to you one more time today, would you tell me what you have been up to?
Would you be doing puzzle books, watching tv, listening to Andy Williams' records, or cooking in the kitchen, making fried bologne sandwiches for eleven people?

I am positive that if I could visit you, it would be so
beautiful beyond words.
I am positive that if I could see you one more time, that the
memory of your hug would envelope me, and surround me
with warmth, love and peace, that I so yearn for.
I am positive that if I could visit you, and that I could
express to you how much that I miss you, you would want
to stay on Earth and fight.

I feel that if I could visit you, we'd be walking hand-in-
hand on a beach in Heaven.
Or perhaps a wooded path with lots of tall trees swaying in
the breeze. It would be warm. I envision Hawaii, or New
Zealand on a summer day, as a backdrop, or perhaps just a
path surrounded by sweet smelling woods and flowers,
with beams of light coming through the branches and
canopies of the trees.

As we would continue to walk, the forest would open up
and low and behold, there would be a cafe waiting for us on
the other side. We would sit. There would be food waiting
for us, with a variety of wines and a centerpiece of flowers
that would take our breaths away.
I would have my three beautiful granddaughters with
me...and I would introduce them to you for the first time,
and you will instantanly fall in love with them, as I have.
You would say, without saying, that they are beautiful and
precious. It would be in your eyes.

We would toast and cling our glasses together, celebrating
our current titles of "Grandmother" and "Great-
grandmother." You would find it in your heart to forgive
my many mistakes, for children represent hope to me and
to you. I see them in me, I see them in you,
I see me in them, I see you in them.

I would see your wonderful smile...and we would talk and
chitchat about unnecessary things, and it would be as if you
had never left.
Dear Mom,
I hope that I haven't disappointed you much.

god's JOKE

What's this?
Where did that blemish come from,
Overnight without warning?
I am not a teenager!

What in the world is that?
It looks like a red string, but no,
The medical profession call them spider veins.
But I am arachnophobic!

Oh my god, what is that?
Seriously, a grey hair, to be exact
A grey eyebrow hair.
It must be plucked.
I am too young for this!

When my grandmother was alive, she was old.
She was plump, with large "shelf breasts,"
And, Oh my goodness...a grey bun!
I look nothing like the grandmothers portrayed
in movies and books!
But, I am a grandmother, all the same.

I should have been told about this!
The importance of exercise,

To ward off the inevitable huge muffin.
Where did these batwings come from?
I am not a nocturnal animal.
Sort of... I just don't sleep well.

What? Another one?
I have hot flashes that show up out of nowhere.
I have cold flashes after the hot flashes,
and must cover up immediately.
I have crow's feet, jowl wrinkles, stretch marks and
Oh my goodness, is that a double chin?
And let's not talk about the "C" word: Cellulite.

Holy crap! Another yeast infection?
I should have taken stock in that OTC medicine.
And, all of a sudden there's a spot on my hand.
They shouldn't be called liver spots, but they
Should be called OMG spots.
Did I get them from drinking some wine?

If these things are inevitable, shouldn't we celebrate them,
as opposed to finding them hideous and revolting?
Why do men want wrinkle-free arm garments,
with perky mams, C-free legs and no muffins?
I will just go find a man who loves
hanging out at the bakery.

I MADE MY BED, NOW I LIE IN IT

During the daylight hours, at work or at play,
I tell myself the truth of truths.
I go about my business, at business, facing the truth about
the incoming and the outgoing, and knowing the rights
from the wrongs, that some things are grey, as much as the
sun shines bright in some sky across some other part
of the world.

But at night, when readying for bed, I stare at the face in
the mirror and I wink, but only for a brief moment, until I
wash off the days exhaustion with soap and water.
A quick shower, bath or not, I don my Pjs, with fluff and
bears, zebra stripes or flowers.
The outside is temporarily dark, but the inside is
permanently dark, if I can help it.
My pillow is lumpy, my bed is way past due...

I made my bed in the morning, as if I was expecting
company. But no one comes to visit.
They are busy, I tell myself.
But no one calls. They are busy, I tell myself.
They forgot my birthday again, they are busy...
A promise of "Let's do lunch," "Let's catch a movie,"
"I'll call you by the weekend."
They are busy with family and other friends, houses to run,
gardens to tend to, errands to run and parties to attend.
He is busy with his adult children, watching sports and
news and whatnot...

But now I lay in my bed, I lie in my bed,
that tomorrow will be better.
They haven't forgotten me, I tell myself.
That tomorrow is a new day, with new possibilities
and that the sun will shine on me.

I pray.
I will meet new friends.
I will meet another some day.
I made my bed, but for now...
I lie in it.

THREE SHIRTS

Here I go again, working too hard, and running
errands in between.
Today is going to be a Three Shirt Day.

I get up, shower and get dressed in tight jeans
and a cute white top with pale flowers on my boobs.
A snazzy belt, a jazzy hairstyle, sandals
and I am on my way.

With purse, small duffle and lunch pail in tow,
it's the chiropractic office, then some grocery shopping,
back home, the post office, then work.

Sitting in my car, it's shirt number two:
a simple blue T, with work logo.
And let's not forget the twisting and turning
to change out sandals to sneakers.
I walk in as if nothing happened.

Eight hours later, work is done,
but my work has yet to begin.
Sitting in my car, it's shirt number three:
a black tight boob shirt, as it were,
and then back to the sandals that completes this ensemble.
Off to the restaurant bar I go, with only purse in tow.

A smile on my face, the day is not quite over.
Shirt number three, as I meet my friend for dinner.
Steak, broccoli, wine and dessert.
And a mighty fine dessert, for this Three Shirt Day.

BACKBONES AND STEPPING STONES, LEFTOVERS AND HAND-ME-DOWNS

Stay focused on what you do right, as opposed to staying over-focused on all that you did wrong.

Obviously, I need to win the lottery or just somehow make more dough in order to get what's required in life, or needed, or wanted, in order to "keep up with the Jones,'" or just to feel normal, or just to be accepted, or at least to blend in...

My list of things to get or do, while I am still alive, because, obviously I can't get them or do them while I'm dead:

*A new mattress (according to those gross commercials, I am way passed due)...
*Health care (first thing that I ask of my blind dates, joking, "You had me a health care!")...
*A better coffee machine (faster caffeine)...
*A sunlamp (being translucent or Casper-like isn't cool)...
*A gym membership (being plump isn't cool)...
*A medieval stretching machine (being short apparently isn't acceptable by some genetically tall men. Screw you, anyway. You're wasting my time!)...
*More makeup and tattooed eyebrows (obviously)...

*Freezing my fat or cellulite removal (ummm, this doesn't even sound healthy)...

*Whiter teeth (perfect Fawcett teeth are trending again. What a beautiful woman she was!)...

*Netflix (to be able to understand what your co-workers are talking about)...

*Regular tv/cable (to be able to understand the politics that your co-workers shouldn't be talking about)...

*Menopause meds (for a calm demeanor. THIS IS NONE OF YOUR CONCERN! I am nice to everyone and everyone knows that)...

*Learn a foreign language (obviously, because this is where the world is turning)...

*New clothes and their unlimited accessories that are fashionable for the upcoming season (okay, this is where I give up...this is not important to me)...

*AAA (this would be nice for road trips)...

*Trendy or popular or brand-named foods and beverages (seriously?)...

*Attend all festivals, concerts, plays, musicals, sports gatherings (this is why I have to stay home)...

*A beau or husband before I die (or I'll be labeled a spinster)...

*Unlimited micro-brew knowledge (Ok! This one I can do!)...

RANDOM THOUGHTS, on this last warm day of the week in October:

*If I was insensitive, I'd be You...
*If I had thick skin, I wouldn't be me, I'd be You...
*If I lied and cheated, I'd be You...
*If I was taller, like you say that you prefer,
I wouldn't be Me...
*If I was skinnier, like you claim that you want,
I wouldn't be Me...
*If I was able to stop the snowball from rolling...or the last straw from falling...or let the water roll off...or if I'd recognize and acknowledge the water under that bridge, in reference to You, I am sure that I could be a better Me.

RANDOM THOUGHTS/RANDOM
QUESTIONS/RANDOM RANTS,
for this "saddish" Wednesday (September, 2016):

*Waking up with a (barometric pressure) headache is the worst...
*The crying all night long thing didn't help either...
*You ask, You ok?:
*My answer is No, but I have faith that I will be...
*Did I mention that menopause sucks?...
*My life's path took another drastic change, so I prefer not to take any more road trips for a while...
*Changing my dreams to none, will free up myself for more focus on more work...
*They say we should not work to live, but instead we should live to work...
*Waiting to exhale, waiting to breathe again...
*Hopefully my wait isn't going to be too long...
*Looking forward to Mondays...

RANDOM FACTS:

*I just don't wear pain very well...
*I look horrible after crying for 5 days...
*I wonder too long of how long this is going to take...
*I fear that I won't recover...
*I need to learn to be selfish...
*I don't understand why I don't understand..
*I am grateful for more than one thing every day...
*I am a good writer...
*I have faith that I'll find my way...
*I've lost weight, unintentionally...
*I want to be a warrior, not a worrier...
*I know now that I am meant to be alone for a while...
*I love my children, my in-laws, and grandchildren...
*I forge onward...
*I have passion, grief, perserverence, faith, compassion, determination...
*I am an empath...
*I wear rose-colored glasses...
*I wear my heart on my sleeve...
*I am an open book...
*I am poor...
*I am exhausted...
*I am alive...

RARE PHOTOS OF GRANDMOTHER, TRUE

That grandmother is caffeinated and running around getting
errands done, with things in tow and a perfectly coiffed
head of perfect hair and her just-enough makeup.
Or so she thinks.

Her selfies are all the rage, from morning jaunts to the
coffee shop, Or just a run to the grocery store, morning,
noon and night. And let's not forget the quick last-minute
selfies of smiles in cars, on the way to or from work, with
the sunlight dancing just so off of her auburn mane.
Oh, and wait, the ones in front of her mirror
or living room window, where she's wearing the dresses
and other outfits that she was just able to get into, after
months of dieting and exercise. A proud size four, indeed.

This is what she presents to the world and to herself, this
perfectly put together Artwork-In-Progress masterpiece of
five feet and zero inches.
Once inside, she is not so perfect, like everyone may think.
She's messy, she has organized clutter, and frequently dons
the "Oh-my-god-look-what-time-it-is" hairstyle of bun,
ponytail, headband. And tons of hairspray.

She doesn't have time to dust, or vacuum, but she does
clean the dishes, the kitchen and bathroom, time permitting,
but mostly in stages that takes three days. Then, it's doing
that all over again the next week. What does this
grandmother really look like, after days of still working too
hard, after days of crying herself to sleep, but only to sleep
for less than the required eight?
What does this grandmother really look like, from the
inside out, with exposed emotions, natural haircolor and
natural hues and tones on her sporadic, speckled, freckled
face?

Her granddaughters see beauty, kindness, playfulness...
with memories of her prized art box, full of crayons, paints,
paper, pens, markers, stickers, glue, ribbons, and assorted
buttons and knick-knacks. With memories of hugs,
macaroni and cheese, allowances of doing dishes while
standing on a chair, long baths with the tub filled to the
brim with toys...dress up in high heels, hats, boas, scarves,
dresses with clothes pins tight against their backs...late
night movies, fingernail polish, and brushing their hair,
after a long day of visiting parks, walks at the mall,
shopping for everything and nothing
and ice cream parlors...

These are the rare photos of grandmother, true to her
selfless self, keeping them safe, thriving, and doting over
the precious ones who will carry on her memory into the
next generation.
Grandmother, truly will be caffeinated again, running
errands for all to see, hiding her sadness of the in-between,
waiting for the next time that she gets to spoil her
grandchildren.

TO MY FRIEND

Dear Friend,

I am dealing with another temporary bout of depression
again, but I have faith that all will be okay. I look forward
to our coorespondences, for your words of faith, hope and
reassurances, helping me get through to the next day.
Your encouraging words I carry with me always. I can
write them down, and literally carry them in my pocket,
looking at them, from time to time, whenever I am in need.
It pleases me about your patience, about your devotion and
dedication and loyalty to me, for I have had many fair-
weathered friends who come and go...and this time they
have all but disappeared. I am not sure where they went.
But they are gone, all the same.

It pleases me, it makes me happy, to know that you do not
judge me, that you do not hang out with me only for your
own selfishness and when things don't go your way, you
won't hang up on me... It pleases me that you won't
abandon me, just because I am no longer needed for that
moment.

I just don't get it, Dear Friend, why someone who claims to
love me, will let me down in my hour of need. I have not
asked for much, of anyone. Why do they only have me
around for temporaries sake, then find others who are that
much more rich, more interesting...and others who will
satisfy whatever they are looking for at that odd moment?
I do not do this, and I was not brought up that way, to
dismiss a friendship, based on other's success, based on my
small jealousy that I admit does exist, or based on what I
think that I know...

Perhaps it is fear. Fear that they think I am something other than what I am not. Perhaps it really is jealousy because now I am doing exactly what I want to do and can do...and they cannot. Perhaps they feel stuck or trapped, and therefore they assume that I possess much more freedom and independence than they do...

I haven't changed. I am richer by means of family and friends, friendship and experiences. Whatever happened to support, cheering on your fellow woman folk, for making successful strides to better themselves, however success is defined, to make improvements that will benefit her, and them, and her & their children and families, and so on? Perhaps it is true, that misery loves company, but when I am not miserable, and I become a bit successful (if that is what this is), I am kicked to the curb, I am given up on...and all forms of communication stops.

Dear Friend, I thank you for your understanding of little old me, of your approval, your no-strings-atttached love and patience. I thank you for accepting me As Is, and for not letting me down. I thank you for letting me cry on your shoulder even if only in letters and emails. Thank you for letting me vent, for listening to my ups and downs...for my unprovoked and unjustified rollercoaster rides, and for not letting me go, despite all of my shortcomings and quirks. Thank you, Dear Friend, for loving me, unconditionally.

SELF-PRESERVATION

I have built another wall around me,
From all the bullshit that I have been dealt.
These walls stink, from all of that bullshit.
I am tired of it, and when I am tired of it,
I am thrown out
And I throw it all out the window.

Isolating myself is a tactic of self-preservation.
I have to work, so I have to deal with coworkers and such.
Makeup is my enemy, but I use it still.
But once I am home, I stay stuck to myself,
Attached to my remote, my computer, my couch
But mostly I stay stuck in bed.

When some energy shows up,
I exercise or bike, walk or hike,
I go see movies by myself,
Which no longer makes me feel like a loser.
I disappear for two hours
And I stick to the theater chair.

I self-preserve, so no one can hurt me.
Again.
Sadly, the ones who hurt me,
Claim to be friendly, loving,
Honest and true.
They are liars and cheaters,
Showing their stripes finally to me.
Perhaps they should be the ones to
Isolate themselves,
And preserve themselves from the world
Around them.

ACTIVELY UNFRIENDLY

I have bent over backwards to help you out,
And therefore I am shocked that I haven't
Been awarded the Gold Medal for Gymnastics.
You claim that I am actively unfriendly,
Without noticing that you are pointing your own fingers
To yourself, and to your own blackened heart.

How could you say such a thing?
For it is you who is the over-exaggerator,
The liar,
The misunderstander,
Over-emphasizing your emotions into this picture
of true daily simplicity.
You should be ashamed.
Your parents would be ashamed.

Try showing up in a better mood.
Try getting out of bed on the right side of it,
Or perhaps try not getting out of bed,
And try to sleep a little longer.
Just like a child, you have a freaking embarressing fit.
A tantrum.
Go take a damn nap.

Splash water on your face,
Find your pretty face.
Smile at your own reflection.
Eat your dessert.
My go-to favorite is always chocolate cake.
Haven't you heard that chocolate releases those
beneficial endorphins?
Or perhaps do other things that release them...

It is much easier in life to be kind and nice,

Than it is to be mean,
To lie,
To slander,
And to be mean-spirited.
Yeah,
Try that.

MEMORY/DEATH

When I die, will you remember me,
As I have you?
Will you remember my quirks and kindnesses,
Will you remember how much laughter that I brought you
And that you have brought me,
And how much I smiled when you were with me?
When you die, I will remember you always,
For your laughter, for the twinkle in your eyes,
Your very love of me, to me, for me.
The memory of your pleasure and touch
Have remained in the DNA of my soul
From the moment we first loved.
It cannot be erased.
It cannot falter.
Your memory cannot disappear,
For it it light,
It is substance,
It is food,
It is energy...
For it is embedded into the very fabric of my body.
Your death will not affect the outcome of the world,
But it will affect the outcome of mine.
You will continue to give it life...

THERE ARE NOT TWO SIDES TO
EVERY ONE-SIDED RELATIONSHIP

I must say that being right all the time
Must be quite exhausting...
I should try that some time,
But I'd hate to be so tired from all of the
Overexaggeration
Of every thing...

I am completely baffled by your acts of kindness
And the retraction of the same kind.
I have yet to understand why I do the things that I do,
Let alone trying to understand your quirks as well.
I only have one side: Kindness mixed with patience,
humor, love, and compassion.

I have yet to understand why I seem to be quite
comfortable in my own skin,
In my own surroundings,
And yours,
Fitting temporarily perfectly into the different molds,
and nook and crannies
Of everyone's lives, domiciles, adventures and such.
Aptly prepared, mind you, with various items in tow...

No one comes to see me, including you, for y'all behave
As if your skin is crawling when you are in my company.
Why is that,
That all of my adventures and experiences begin with
others and ends with just the same?

You don't call or contact,
Because you don't care.
This has always been quite obvious to the Outside me,
But I've been too damn scared to let this

one-sided-ness go...
Fear overtakes the inside me,
who is screaming and crying silently.

Why is that?
Why do you behave as if you are just that damn busy,
When everyone knows that you're not?
Including you...
And yet, there you are, spending time and efforts
with others.

It's a hard chunk to swallow,
Knowing that this one-sided relationship
has always leaned to your Right,
Then, with that lean, comes me falling when I am Left.
I am letting go now, whereas I am floating
To a much better place where there are not two sides.

THE PROMISE OF FOREVER

When does my promise of forever come?
It seems that cookie-cutter women have the promise,
Despite looking happy, when I am sure that they are not.
The promise comes to those who have
Something other than patience to give.
Something other than kindness to offer,
Something other than a hand to hold.
That promise comes with strings, it seems.
With memories that I have not forged,
With memories of me that are soon forgotten.
But my strings stretch around the Earth fourfold,
Until the moment that they snap.
Where does this promise reside?
In the four corners of forever and nothing.

JUNE, JULY, AUGUST OPTIONS

June: Shorts, tanks, push-ups and sandals, capris, newly
cut bobs and fake tans. Cookouts, workouts, gym
memberships unused, outdoor running, outdoor sports,
preparations for upcoming holidays, the dumping of love...

July: More shorts but shorter, more tanks but more
spaghetti-er, pools and sunscreen. Surgery to enlarge and
enhance, flip-flops, highlights, and wrinkling skin.
Celebrations, fireworks, vacations and higher gas prices,
heated arguments, not enough shade...

August: Capris and jeans, short-sleeved shirts, movies and
popcorn, exercise garb, sneakers, longer manes, more
cookouts, sailing, more sports, more arguments, and jackets
for the upcoming colder weather...

THE CEILING FAN

I am lying on the living room floor again...
staring at the ceiling fan. I wonder where this was
manufactured, and I wonder if the person who assembled
this lives in a foreign country with no walls, no air, a dirt
floor and sparce clothing, making ten cents a day, and
starving.

I have to wonder why this has popped into my head again,
as I wonder about other's lives and what they have been
through.
I am lying on the living room floor...
I stare at the Mellow Lime painted north-facing brick wall,

and I wonder who built it, and if this person, is living on a
tropical island, happy in the knowledge of his trade, as he is
watching the sunset while drinking a margarita.

I can hear the hard footsteps above me, the mumbling
and the accidental slamming of doors, entering from a long
day at work. My casement windows rattle from the
activity. I can hear the footsteps become lighter, imagining
that the ceiling above, and the floor below them, would be
made of glass, as I watch their day unfold.

I wonder about these loud creatures, as then unwind, as
they turn on their TV and eat dinner, and as they discuss
their day with each other. I can hear the changing of the
channels, the walks to the kitchen where they get seconds
and more to drink. I have no idea of their names, or of
what they do during the day, but, at this moment, late at
night, the roar becomes louder, and I can hear them mating
again, on my ceiling.

I am lying on the living room floor, again...
exhausted from the days shameful earnings, too tired to lift
my head, let alone lift my lifeless mind, with enough
energy to actually get into my own bed. The day's clothing
remains on, with the stink of my own disappointment
again. I wonder about myself and from where I came...
And from what factory I had been manufactured.

SENSE OF ENTITLEMENT

Why can't you just know that you are not entitled
To the air that you breathe?
I know, and I was taught so.
Your sense is interferring with my sense of compassion
And the obvious sense of right from wrong.
You have proved time and time again,
That you think that you are a gift to me, whereas,
Sir, it is the other way around.
You are not entitled to anything,
More than I am entitled to speak my mind.
You have no sense of real humor,
Whereas your humor is daggers at me,
Meant to hurt me, with the lies of "I am just kidding,"
Coming at me, time and time again.
My neck hurts from all the dodging.
I am convinced that all of you have graduated
From the same schools,
Where the lessons of being insensitive,
But thinking that your are priviledged,
Are being taught, from the day that you were born.

JUMPING OVER THE BETRAYAL HURDLE

Boy, Oh boy, do I ever get my exercise,
As I jump again over that hurdle of betrayal.
I need to hit the gym, or just use my own
equipment in my home,
Exercising daily, on my treadmill, trampoline,
and using my weights,
To strengthen my mind, and regrowing my spine.
I need to grow snakeskin, but snakes cannot jump.
Snakes slither.
They charm, then they strike.
I need to buy some new sneakers, and start running,
Especially when I see that hurdle coming into focus.

SHORT

What is the deal with you mentioning
About me being short?
I am not that short, but for Pete's sake,
You mention it frequently.
You are not all that, or all that tall.
And answer me this, Do I make fun of you...to your face?
I am sure that you have some vertically-challenged friends,
But never mention their lack of height, to them or me.
Or do you have friends?
So why do you feel such the need to successfully
Attempt to belittle me?
No pun intended.
For a rise?
No pun intended.
So you caught me in your kitchen using a spatula
To get something out of your upper cabinet,

While I was climbing your kitchen counter.
Laughing about this for over a week is quite overkill.
Get over it...
You use sentences of intended destruction,
With words of "shortcomings," "short-changed,"
And "little time," "smidgen," "small-minded," etc...
If my height bothers you so much,
Don't bother me.
You are the one who is small-minded.
Despite your height, you are the smallest of us all.

DAILY TRUTH

The thing is...
I am always an open book, with a crooked spine,
A dusty hardback cover, aging chapters, and fading pages.
I think that it is way past time to keep to myself.
I think that my book is quite overdue.

The thing is...
Since we are all connected, perhaps what I am feeling isn't
just my pain.
It is yours, too, and everyone else all across the universe.
I feel myself flying past you, trying to grab your hand
and hold on.
I think that it is way past time for me to stop flying.
I think that my pilot's license has expired.

The thing is...
Somedays, being an empath, is just too painful to bear.
I am like an antenna, capturing the cries and the silent
screams of everyone.
I'd like to trade in my personality for a
two-dimensional character.
I think that it is way past time for me to stop creating.
I think that it's time that my wave-length stops waving.

BOX CUTTER

I am spending too much time alone,
with my racing thoughts,
She said,
And thoughts that show up uninvited, out of nowhere.
I'd like to take a box cutter to my carotid,
Every time he pops into my head,
And cut out the pain, so I can see it,
Reason with it, and ask it to kindly leave.

I could be doing dishes...
I could be doing laundry...
I could be sitting on the pot doing my business...
And there the pains show up.

And there he shows up, leaving again, cheating again,
Lying again, and looking happier than when I saw him last.
I'd like to take a box cutter to my wrists,
She said,
Every time these memories or visions rear up.

Or if the notion shows up,
To buy a cat, or a dog,

Whom I'd love to love,
But can't afford to take care of...
My lonliness goes that deep,
That I'd consider getting a pet
To have around, to lessen my misery.

I'm sure my cat would be okay at my home,
alone, for hours,
As I work my three jobs, while he rests on my bed.
My cat would get into all of my things, but that'll be okay,
I've got nothing to hide.
The dog, however, would have to be small,
Not able to jump onto my bed.
He'd probably get into my things on the floor
And under the bed, but that's okay, too,
She said.
The smaller the dog,
The smaller the sass,
The smaller the poop,
And the smaller the food.

As this stream of thought flows,
I think of taking a box cutter to my gut,
Hoping these stupid thoughts stop flowing,
Out of nowhere, inflicting me from out of the universe
from whence it came.
This cut would spill out my pains
And possibly disappear forever.

I'd like to take a box cutter to my neck,
She said,
To end these unprovoked thoughts that hit my
consciousness,
Causing immediate sadness, and embarrassing tears.
It's embarrassing, even when alone at home.
Especially thoughts of him, when the wrong,

Or the right, song starts on my radio.

I've drowned without being in water.
I've drowned while laying in bed.
I've drowned while driving.
I feel myself falling downward,
Unable to stop the spiral,
Unable to hold onto any edge of this vicious circle.

The person who commits suicide
is not the one being selfish,
But the one who want them not to, is.
As I see myself fall, I'm able to grab one thing,
She said...
As I try to stop myself from hitting the ground
with full force,
Smashing my frail body into thousands of puzzle pieces,
Which can never be reassembled in this lifetime...

Of all of my choices, whether it be a rope, a wrench,
A bench, or a compliment,
I hope the one thing that I can grab, is a box cutter,
She said.

SO WHAT DO YOU MEAN BY THAT?

Why is it that when someone makes a joke at my expense,
I cannot take that joke and slough it off, like the dandruff
That's on his shoulders, that I want to tell him about
And remind him that he, too, has faults and problems?

Why is it that when someone makes a joke at my expense,
I still have not grown thick skin, after all this time,
Like that snake that he is, that I want to tell him that
Slithering and being mean-spirited are not good qualities?

Why is it that when someone makes a joke at my expense,
I cower, and cannot come up with a zinger and a great one-
liner, as a grand comeback, to attack and demean,
and to tell him exactly what is on my mind, about him,
even if minutes later?

I don't, because I know it is wrong.

Why is it that when someone makes a joke at my expense,
I have to remind myself, in my head, that not all people
Are kind and gentle souls, like myself, that I want to tell
him that making a joke at my expense is more about who
he is, than who I am?...

And I dare not ask, "So what do you mean by that?"
For when I would, I would get more jokes at my expense.

UNDERLINE

My underline is childhood issues of being fat,
Being made fun of for being fat,
And continuously being up and down fat, as an adult.
And being made fun of as an adult for being fat.

People are cruel.
Was I a cruel child, and now, somehow,
it is underline payback time?
I cannot remember being a cruel child,
or making fun of people at all.

My underline is childhood issues of lack of trust, whereas
My brothers and perhaps even my dad, would come up
behind me,
And deliberately scare the crap out of me, figuratively,
So now, I don't like people directly behind me.
Unless I asked them to be there.

People don't think.
Was I an unthoughtful child, and now, somehow it is
underline payback time?

My underline is adult issues of partings,
Sometimes on a mass scale, too hard for me to
comprehend,
That perhaps started somewhere in my childhood,
None of which I can currently recall.
People come and go, but for me, mostly, they go,
But only after they have been upsetting and show
previously hidden scales.

People disappear.
Perhaps I was a disappearing child, and now, somehow it is
underline payback time...

VARIOUS STAGES OF DECOMPOSITION

This time of year is the worst,
as I have more time to reflect and ruminate,
And realize that I've not improved much
over the years of alone-liness.
This feeling sorry for myself thing, at these intervals,
Is hard to shake, at this time of year.
Autumn, which leads into the cold, and obvious darkness
Of heartless winters...

My sadnesses peel off my Hope, one moment at a time,
Not unlike the peeling of sunburned Irish skin,
Which has had too much exposure to the summer sun.
Reminders of being alone, with commercials that incite
Tears and sadness, are just about everywhere.
Couples holding hands, as I walk and hike past them
On the trails and paths, in the early mornings
and even late at night,
And, Oh for Pete's sake!...even
In the damn grocery store.
Get a room!

I do have faith that I'll be okay,
But apparently my body and brain needs sunshine
24/7/365...
And temperatures above eighty degrees.
Don't get me wrong.
Despite my verbal rantings, I do muster up a smirk,
Or even a smile, as I think of holding the hand
of a strong man.
I am truly, overall, definitely, unconditionally Happy
For the passing couples that I do not want to run into...

The reality is that I cannot afford to move,
But equal is the reality that I cannot afford Not to move.

Somewhere south would be nice, where the sunshine
Would improve my life tremendously.
I think that this evil is called Seasonal Affected Disorder,
SAD, if you will, and how aptly named.

But admitting that I have a disorder
should come easy for me.
But it doesn't come easy.
I still have to function, to work, to live.
But this lack of sunshine, and these daily barometric
pressure headaches,
Are killing me, and causing various stages of
decomposition
While I am still awake and alive.

From the moment that I was born, I have been dying.
From the moment that I had gotten involved with a guy,
here and there,
Seven years after my divorce,
I've been dying, with these various
Stages of decomposition.
These peelings should do the opposite,
Exposing the truths that all men are not scum,
liars and cheaters,
With whom I allowed myself to get involved.
But, alas, No,
I attract the scum, whom have contributed to
My decomposition.

My decomposition should be visible, and obvious,
And un-appealing to the naked eye
Of men, but for some reason, they are deliberately
blind to it.
Or perhaps, they are not so blind.
I believe that their various stages of decomposition
Are hidden behind their masks of compliments that

They throw out like candy to parade-goers.
Telling me what I think that I want to hear,
Telling me what I crave to hear, masking lies
With untruths that add to my various stages
Of decomposition.

SWORDS AND ARROWS

You aim your swords and arrows at my castle.
My head has lots of holes in it.
Out of those holes comes my thoughts
of how to help heal you.
But you may not be worth it.
You jab your swords and arrows at my back.
My spine has many knicks and wounds.
Out of those wounds comes my hopes and dreams...
But are they worth saving?
You stab your swords and arrows at my heart.
My soul has become blackened from your rust.
Out of that blackness comes my unconditional love for you.
My love is worthy, and as strong as my
Swords and arrows.

EVERYONE LOOKS LIKE BOB,
FOR HE SET THE TONE

Oh my word, again, I ran into Bob.
Just didn't understand why he was such a slob.
He's not just a noun, but he's also a verb.
And why couldn't his name be something like Herb?

His lying set the pace, and set my soul afire.
Too bad he couldn't be one who would just inspire.
I've come not to trust, thinking all are bad to the bone.
Everyone looks like Bob, for he set the tone.

I must say that I feel sorry for his current wife,
I am sure that she too is suffering from his strife.
He doesn't know that I know that she
Has also cheated on him,
Perhaps that's because that he too wanted her too slim.

He looked like the number zero, just plump and round.
I now know that his shallow mind was not quite sound.
For how could he not have loved me rightly?
It was my family, that he felt was too unsightly.

Mine was large, his much smaller, and so it seems,
That his mind was shut off from all of my dreams.
I wanted bigger, larger, and grander, and brighter,
Times of travel, and experiences, for I am a fighter.

I see me sailing oceans, and hiking mountains galore,
I know I will have that, for I am deserving of more.
He was content in his surroundings,
Staying shielded in his house.
He just really didn't see me, and wanted me
Quiet as a mouse.

He just didn't know me,
And didn't realize that I am dynamic.
If he admitted his mistake,
That would give him such a panic.
Keep to yourself, Bob, for you are as blind as a bat.
Know that I am doing just fine without you,
And that is just that.

SANS-A-BEAU

I am inventing a new holiday, for singles,
called Sans-A-Beau.
This holiday will be celebrated every weekend,
Especially around the other coupled and familial holidays.

Anyone can celebrate, with spur-of-the-moment
Gatherings, with food and drinks abounding.
Especially alcohol.

I am creating greeting cards right now,
Garnished with glitter, and pictures of singles,
at dinner, in bars,
Riding rollercoasters and going to the movies,
Especially, unashamed and singly.

Commercials are forecoming, with blind date events,
Cookouts, mall-brousing, golf outings, birthday parties,
And especially conveying the continuous disappointments,
Of friends who cancel.

Cupcakes and pretzels, chips and dips,
Microwave meals, and grocery shopping, for one.
Making dinner and freezing the leftovers,

Especially, to thaw and eat after midnight, the next night.

Oh, and let's not forget all the accoutrements
That will be created from this holiday,
Like various clothing, handbags, coffee mugs,
Jewelry, picture frames, pottery,
And a Sans-A-Beau tree,
From which one can swing...

CONFETTI AND RICE

I want edible confetti in my rice,
In my meals,
Colorful and tasty.
I want confetti and rice,
To pop up every time I rise from sleep,
Glittery and shiny.
I want confetti and rice
To pour from my daily shower,
Warm and soothing.
I want confetti
To be tossed my way, as soon as I get to work.
In celebration of me.
I want confetti and rice,
Since I didn't get rice and confetti.

I am blessed to have such wonderful "personal cheerleaders" in my life:

My children, Craig and Claire, my son-in-law Joshua, my daughter-in-law Marta, my 3 beautiful granddaughters, and of course, my friends, my Dad and my family.

If it wasn't for their support and encouragement, their positive words which added excitement to my writing, and the ocassional crying and laughing, I may have stopped writing altogether.

They have given me things to think about, and they have helped me stay on track. They have encouraged me to travel, take risks, try new things, or just stay home (and write) in my hometown of Dayton, Ohio.

I am in AWE of their lives, with its hardships, struggles and its accomplishments.

I am in AWE of mine, as well. I am blessed to have them in my life and take them along on this wonderful journey.